Uinta Rock

Cover: Jeff Baldwin on the 1st ascent of Adore 5.11a. Photo: Nathan Smith

Inside cover: Susan Bown on Steiner Arete V0. Photo: Nathan Smith

Uinta Rock, A Guide to Climbing on the Mirror Lake Scenic Byway

By Nathan Smith & Paul Tusting

Printed in the United States of America

ISBN: 0-9755299-0-0

Authors: Nathan Smith, Paul Tusting
Layout & Design by: Nathan Smith
Map/topo design and all uncredited photos: Nathan Smith
Illustrations: Kevin Rogers

Send comments, suggestions or any information concerning climbing in the Uintas to:
info@pullpublishing.com

Published and distributed by:
Pull Publishing, LLC.
PO Box 526337
Salt Lake City, UT 84152-6337

Pull Publishing is looking for new ideas and manuscripts for books. Please contact us at the e-mail or address above.

Uinta Rock

Uinta Rock

A Guide to Climbing on the Mirror Lake Scenic Byway

By
Nathan Smith
Paul Tusting

Uinto Rock

Introduction

WARNING!
CLIMBING IS DANGEROUS! YOU MAY FACE DEATH, DISFIGUREMENT, OR SERIOUS INJURY IF YOU DECIDE TO CLIMB THE ROUTES REPRESENTED IN THIS BOOK. READ THIS BEFORE YOU USE THIS BOOK!

Rock climbing is inherently dangerous and any involvement in the activity could result in serious injury or death. The information contained within this guide is compiled from many different sources, and the authors cannot guarentee the accuracy of the information including but not limited to: topos, drawings, maps, directions, route descriptions, bolt counts, gear selection, length of climb, grades, seriousness ratings, objective dangers, safety of fixed protection and access issues. If you are not willing to assume complete responsibility for your own actions and life, then DO NOT use this book or the information contained within.

The publisher and authors expressly disclaim all representations and warranties regarding this guide, the accuracy of the information contained herein, and the results of your use hereof, including without limitation, implied warranties of merchantability and fitness for a particular purpose. The user assumes all risk associated with the use of this guide.

If you use this guide and the information contained within, you are taking your life into your own hands. You face real danger. Be smart, be safe, use this guide for what it was meant for, a reference for you to make your own decisions and opinions concerning your safety. If you have any doubts about you ability to safely climb any of the routes represented in this book, do not even try to climb. Seek expert training and instruction. This is not an instructional manual.

REMEMBER, ONLY YOU ARE RESPONSIBLE FOR YOUR ACTIONS.

4

Thanks and Dedication - Nathan:

Cheri Smith – When I first decided to work on this guide, I never realized how much of my life this would consume. Through all the trips to the Uintas, the long hours spent in front of a computer and the thousands of dollars spent in order to make this happen, Cheri has been there for me. I cannot thank you enough.
Love,

Nate

Paul Tusting – Without Paul's time and support this book would only be a fraction of what it is today. From exploring new areas to belaying me for hours while developing new routes to just being there for my endless questions. Thanks for all your help.

Climbing Partners:
Cheri Smith, Tom Adams, Heath Christensen, Joi Rigby, Brian Poulson, Mike Haag, Jeff Baldwin, Tom Nay, Tessie Rose, Matt Sherry, Greg Thompson, Britton Woolfe, Addy Sage, Susan Bown, Kevin Rogers, Chad Jolley, Ed Fallis, Tom Hore, John Rogers, Harry Adelson, Ann Dartnel, Ryan McDermott, and Jared Campbell.

Route Developers:
These people not only donated their time and knowledge of the Uintas, but have also spent countless hours and thousands of dollars establishing the routes in this book:
Jeff Baldwin, Rip Griffith, Brian Cabe, Ray Dahl, Jonny Woodward, Jim Stone, Fred Henion, James Taylor, Chris Harmston, Doug Heinrich, Dave Smith and John Rogers. Paul Moore & Shane Willet: although they are no longer with us, their legacy remains.

Tech Support:
Matt Sherry, Drew Cain, Tim McAllister, Greg Thompson, and Jared "The Pad" Campbell. Stephanie and crew at Ferrari Color, Wasatch Photographic and everyone at Paragon Press.

Advertisers:

Without the support of the following businesses this book would not have been possible. Please remember to support them whenever possible.

Black Diamond, Black Diamond Retail, Docere Clinics, IME, Liberty Mountain, Omega Pacific, Petzl and the Samak Smoke House.

I'd like to dedicate this book to the men and women of the Salt Lake County Search and Rescue. This team of volunteers sacrifice their time, gear and energy in order to help others. I'd also like to thank Chad Wahlquist, Jason Cutler, and many others that were there for us. Words can never do justice in finding ways to thank you. Please know that Cheri and I will never forget you.

Thanks and Dedication – Paul:

I would like to thank the climbers who introduced me to developing new routes; Chris Harmston, Jonny Woodward, and Doug Heinrich. I could have found good adventures by myself, but the things they have taught me make sure I get home. Not many people get to share a rope with their childhood heroes.

I would also like to dedicate this guide to the memory of my dear friend Sean Spinney. You are with us in spirit and are missed.

← Dr. Harry Adelson N.D., naturopathic physician in Salt Lake City and Park City and the Director of Medical Services to the Professional Climbers Association, Will Help Get You Back on the Rock with Mesotherapy and Prolotherapy.

Don't let pain or injury keep you off the rock!

Naturopathic Pain Medicine—Real Medicine for Real Athletes

When you've experienced a climbing injury, why not see a doctor who's experienced in treating climbers.

FOR MORE INFORMATION CONTACT:
801-582-3260
OR VISIT www.docereclinics.com

DOCERE CLINICS

Uinta Rock

Index

Uinta Rock

Introduction

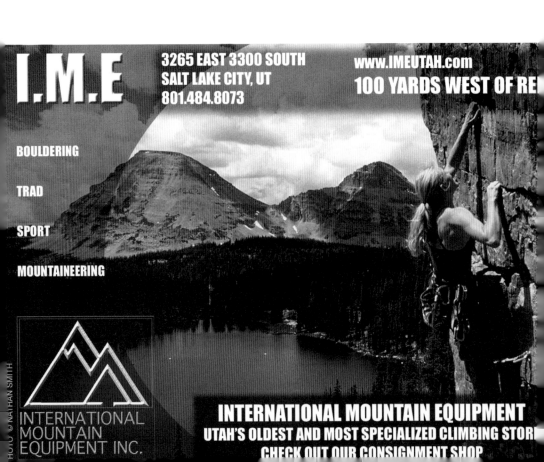

Gold! The Uinta range in Utah is full of it! From Aztec gold carried into the Uintas by Montezuma's royal bearers fleeing from Cortez in the 1500's, to Spanish mines worked by enslaved Native Americans in the 1700's to secret caves hidden in the mountains full of endless gold veins. But unfortunately legends, tall tales and a host of books are the only evidence of the existence of this gold. Many have searched for the elusive gold in the hills but none have found it…until now.

As early as the late 60's prospectors began to search for the elusive mother lode. These pioneers made a few hits here and there, but the rich veins eluded them until a small band of prospectors hit the first mother lode in 1995. Hidden around 10,000 feet behind a shroud of pines and aspens and just minutes off the Mirror Lake Scenic Byway lies the modern day rock prospector's dream. The Stone Garden, a cliff band up to 75 feet tall with 24 routes from 5.7 to 5.12d and angles from just off-vertical to the steepest lines around. Eureka! Fool's gold!

The discovery of great rock just 1 1/2 hours from Salt Lake City in one of the most scenic settings around has given locals "gold fever" and development has been fast paced. There are now over 20 separate areas and almost 400 routes in this amazing high altitude ecosystem. While summer temperatures reach the triple digits in the Salt Lake valley, temps in the Uintas are typically 20-30 degrees cooler. Add the cool temps with scenic forests of pine and aspen, craggy peaks reaching over 13,000 feet and hundreds of beautiful alpine lakes and it's no wonder that locals have been heading for the high country in droves.

General Information:

Season

The Uintas are a summer area with temps typically 20-30 degrees cooler than the Salt Lake Valley. Depending on snowpack, the Mirror Lake Scenic Byway opens on Memorial Day Weekend and remains open until November/December. Lower areas such as the Recess and Portal can be accessed as early as April, but can often be wet. Snowdrifts can cover the trail in June, but the cliffs and talus at the base of the climbs are usually dry at the south-facing crags. July and August are prime months, and September-October can still be bearible as long as you dress warmly.

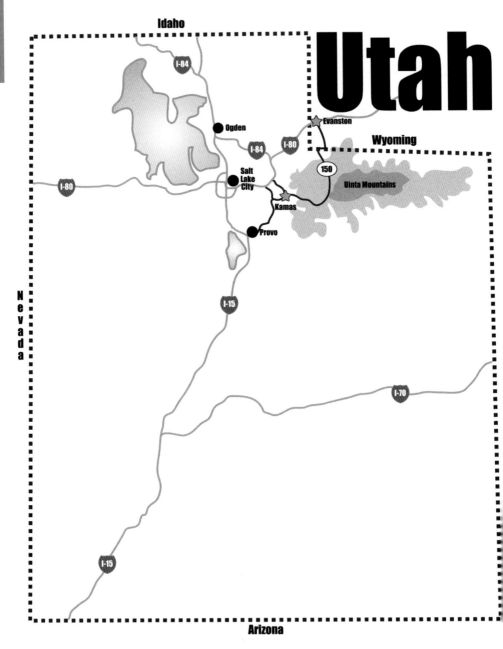

Idaho

Utah

Evanston

Wyoming

Ogden

I-84 I-80

Salt
Lake
City

150 Uinta Mountains

I-80

Kamas

Provo

N
e
v
a
d
a

I-15

I-70

I-15

Arizona

Rock

Mix the hard compactness of quartzite with the texture of granite (but nicer on the skin), throw in the look of sandstone and you have Uinta quartzite. The rock is highly featured and horizontal cracks tend to run uniformly along entire cliff bands. While there are vertical cracks for gear, most placements are in these horizontal bands. The geology of the area tends to keep the cliffs vertical, but a few steeper exceptions occur.

Routes and Grades

The Uintas are a moderate climbers dream. With the majority of routes weighing in around 5.10 and under, the Uintas have something for everyone. Routes vary from short 25 footers to multipitch alpine adventures. Sport climbers will enjoy the predominately bolted Jax, Moosehorn, and Ruth Lake, while those willing to place gear will enjoy the Recess, Portal, Wall of Tiers and Scout Lake. For those seeking harder lines, head to the Stone Garden to find the steepest rock in the Uintas.

Driving Directions:

From Salt Lake City:
Take I-80 Eastbound to exit 148, US-40 toward Heber/Vernal. Follow US-40 for 3.8 miles then exit on exit 4. Turn left onto UT-248 (Eastbound) and drive 11.4 miles. Turn left onto UT-32/S Main St. in Kamas. Drive 0.2 miles then turn right (Eastbound) on UT-150/E Center St (Mirror Lake Scenic Byway). Approximate drive time from SLC to Mirror Lake 1 hour, 20 min.

From Ogden:
Take I-84 Eastbound (approximately 40 miles) to exit 120, I-80 Westbound toward Salt Lake for 11.8 miles then exit on exit 156. Turn right onto E Wanship Rd/UT-32 for 0.1 miles then turn left to stay on E Wanship Rd/UT-32. Drive for 0.2 miles then turn left onto Main St/UT-32. Follow UT-32 for 15.9 miles into Kamas. Turn left onto UT-150/E Center St (Mirror Lake Scenic Byway). Approximate drive time from Ogden to Mirror Lake 2 hours.

From Provo:
Take N University Ave/US-189 through Provo Canyon for 27.2 miles.

Turn left onto S Main St/US-40/US-189. Follow US-40 for 4.7 miles then turn right onto UT-32. Follow UT-32 for 10.3 miles then turn left onto UT-32/N Main Francis for 2.2 miles into Kamas. Turn right onto UT-150/E Center St (Mirror Lake Scenic Byway). Approximate drive time from Provo to Mirror Lake 1 hour 40 minutes.

From Evanston:
Take exit 5 off of I-80 and onto Front St/WY-150 Southbound. Follow WY-150 approximately 46.7 miles to Mirror Lake. Approximate drive time from Evanston to Mirror Lake 1 hour 10 minutes.

Directions to cliffs:
The maps and area descriptions in this guide have mileage starting at the tollbooth which is approximately 6.3 miles from Kamas. We have also tried to include all mile marker information to help those entering from Evanston.

Climbing History:

The known history of climbing in the Uintas is a bit lacking. From the 1960's to the early 1990's development was very slow and consisted mainly of single trad routes here and there. Many of these lines were established around Camp Steiner by the camp councilors. The earliest known climber was Dave Smith in 1968. Unfortunately today, Dave does not remember many of the lines he established. He has stated that unless it was an obvious crack that could take passive gear about 5.8 or under, he did not climb it. While this is consistent with the times, we believe that there is a bit of modesty in this statement and harder lines may have been done.

Some of the other notable climbers from Camp Steiner have been: Ray Dahl, Kevin Rogers and James Taylor who over the years have established many good lines in the Steiner area.
There is evidence at many of the crags in this guide that others have established lines that have been long forgotten. Fixed stoppers, pitons, old bolts and faded webbing have been found at the top of many supposed first ascents. Hopefully we will be able to learn more about the history of the area for future editions of this guide.

Quiet development continued until the early 90's when there was a flurry of new route development. In 1995 The Stone Garden was discovered and developed by a small group of friends. Paul

Moore, Mark Nakada and Shane Willet led the charge and with some help from Jonny Woodward developed the area in one summer. The following summer the group moved on to Ruth Lake and along with Jim Stone started development. In two years the group developed almost 40 climbs with close to 20 of these developed by Jim Stone. Rip Griffith worked on filling in many of the trad lines and a few other filled in the rest. As available lines at Ruth Lake dwindled, a new area was discovered.

The Summer of 1998 saw Paul Moore, Mark Nakada and Shane Willet moving on to develop the Moosehorn area. In the past, the development of areas had been kept quiet and held mainly to a small group of climbers, but the Moosehorn saw many others helping in the development. Again, Rip Griffith worked on plugging the cracks while Dough Heinrich and Drew Bedford established many of the hardest lines at the Moosehorn. Brian Cabe and John Evans worked on establishing many moderates on the cliffs below the main Moore Wall.

Meanwhile a few miles down the road development began anew at the Book Cliffs above Scout Lake. Nathan Smith along with Kevin Rogers began to develop many new routes and boulder problems. Many of these lines were established slowly as a hand drill was the only available means to bolt. Around this time Jim Stone published the first guide to the area and the Uintas popularity as a summer climbing destination started to rapidly grow. Tragically, during the summer of 1998, Paul Moore died in a car accident on the Mirror Lake Scenic Byway while heading back home, after a day of climbing.

While the three main sport climbing areas (The Moosehorn, Ruth Lake and The Stone Garden) received much traffic, others began the search for new areas. More then half of the routes in the Uintas have been developed within the last six years. Jonny Woodward has remained prolific in his development. In the strict British ethic of "ground up" and no fixed gear, Jonny has had a hand in developing lines at The Recess, The Portal and Lovenia Lake.

In 2000, Chris Harmston and Paul Tusting began developing the Murdock Basin area and established many great "adventure" climbs. In 2001 the Wall Lake Area, Fehr Lake, Lovenia Lake and the beginning of The Wall of Tiers saw development. Rip Griffith along with Fred Henion developed Fehr Lake while Paul Tusting started working the Wall Lake Area. Jeff Baldwin published *A Rock Climbing Guide to the Uintas* which contaned many of the recently developed areas.

In 2002 Paul Tusting continued to explore and develop many new areas while Rip Griffith and Fred Henion brought in Chris Harmston and Paul Tusting to continue development of The Wall of Tiers. Nathan Smith developed the Notch Lake Wall as well as added new lines at Jax Cliff and Ruth Lake. Jeff Baldwin added a few quality lines at Ruth Lake as well as new lines at Castle Lake. Bryan Beavers and a Black Diamond crew developed the Chopping Block and Tobacco Wall at Castle Lake.

The 2003 season had more emphasis on completing projects as opposed to developing new areas. The Wall of Tiers received the most attention, although projects were wrapped up at cliffs all over the Mirror Lake Scenic byway. The one exception was Brian Cabe's development of Cliff Lake.

As this guide goes to print new routes and areas are being developed at a quick pace. As long as climbers continue to minimize their impacts. The history of climbing in the Uintas should continue to flourish.

Kamas Diner Guide

Unlike most gateway cities, Kamas has not succumbed to the evils of the chain restaurant. What you sacrifice in speed is MORE than made up for with great food and great service in small family style restaurants. You'll be hard pressed to go wrong with any of the following eateries.

Dicks - 235 E. Center St. ~ 60's style burger joint with great burgers and shakes.

Gateway Grille - 215 S. Main ~ A contemporary menu with something for everyone.

Hi-Mountain Drug - Grill/Sporting Goods - 40 N. Main ~ Old fashioned grill with old fashioned service.

Kamas Cafe - 35 S. Main ~ A classic small town cafe. Try the apple pie.

Pasillas - 185 S. Main ~ Southwestern menu with dishes for vegetarians and carnivores alike. Dinner here is worth the drive alone.

Provisions - Coffee/Deli ~ On Main, next to the Chevron.

Summit Inn - 80 S. Main ~ Home-style pizza with huge portions.

Supplies/Groceries

Chevron - Corner of Main and the Mirror Lake Highway
Hi-Mountain Drug - Grill/Sporting Goods - 40 N. Main
Hoyt's Ace Hardware
Kamas Auto Service - (435) 783-6550
Kamas Food Town - 145 W. 200 S. - Groceries, ATM
Kamas Theater - Movies
Key Bank - ATM
Phillips 66 ~ Mountain Valley Convenience Store -
Poison Creek Antiques/Art Gallery
Samak Smoke House & Country Store - Amazing jerky,
smoked meats and sandwiches - 1937 Mirror Lake Highway,
see page 65.
TR's Auto Repair 24-hr Towing (435) 783-4304
(435) 640-2746
Uinta Auto Parts ~ Parts Plus
Utah State Liquor Agency - 175 S. Main, just left of Pasillas.
Zions Bank - ATM

Guide Service

White Pine Touring - (435) 649-8710 or
www.whitepinetouring.com

Climbing Shops

Black Diamond Retail - 2084 East 3900 South, Salt Lake City.
(801) 278-5552 or www.blackdiamondequipment.com/store
IME - 3265 East 3300 South, Salt Lake City. (801) 484-8073 or
www.imeutah.com
White Pine - 1685 Bonanza Drive, Park City. (435) 649-8710 or
www.whitepinetouring.com

Uinto Rock

Contact Info

Introduction

The Access Fund
P.O. Box 17010
Boulder, CO 80908
(303) 545-6772
www.accessfund.org

Wasatch-Cache National Forrest
Supervisors Office
125 South State Street
Salt Lake City, UT 84138
(801) 524-5030
www.fs.fed.us/r4/wcnf/

Kamas Ranger District
50 East Center Street
P.O Box 68
Kamas, UT 84036
(435) 783-4338

Evanston Ranger District
1565 E. Highway 150 S.
Evanston, WY 82931
(307) 789-3194

EMERGENCY 911
Summit County Sheriff (435) 783-4356
Utah Highway Patrol (801) 576-8606

To Report Fires (801) 908-2000
(435) 370-8930

For fishing information (435) 783-4883

For road conditions (435) 783-4502

Salt Lake Climbers Alliance
info@saltlakeclimbers.org
www.saltlakeclimbers.org

Rest Day Activities
Tour the Kamas Fish Hatchery (435) 783-4883 Open 8am to 4pm.
To volunteer with the Kamas Ranger District call: (435) 783-4338

Mountain Biking - See *Mountain Biking Utah's Wasatch & Uinta Mountains* by Gregg Bromika
Hiking - See *High Uinta Trails* by Davis & Veranth or *High Uintas Backcountry* by Jeffrey & Brad Probost

Weather:
Afternoon thunderstorms frequently form in the Uintas. It can go
from 80 degrees to 30 degrees in minutes. Rain, sleet, hail and snow
are all possible even on the hottest summer days, (some days might
see all four.) Make sure you keep a light rain jacket and light insulation
in your pack. Lightning can also be an issue. Since 1950, there have
been 51 deaths and 131 injuries in Utah, due to lightning. If you do
encounter lightning avoid the following areas:
- Summits and ridges.
- Open areas, meadows.
- Lakes, ponds, rivers.
- Lone tall objects such as a tree.
Find a dense stand of trees that are even in height. If in a group,
spread out to reduce the likelihood of everyone being struck. Be sure
to keep distance between you and your climbing gear. Try to put
something that is non-conductive beneath you and make yourself as
small as possible.

Elevation
All the climbing areas described in this guide are situated between
7,000 and 12,000 feet in elevation. The drastic change in altitude
from Salt Lake or areas even lower in elevation can lead to hypoxia
or altitude sickness. Some of the possible symptoms include fatigue,
nausea and headaches. Much of this can be avoided by drinking
plenty of water and pacing yourself. If you do feel sick, head to lower

elevations immediately.

Another hazard of the high altitude is the sun. As the atmosphere is thinner there is less filtering of the suns rays. Make sure you have sunscreen and sunglasses.

Mosquitos

As the snow melts, shallow pools of water form providing the perfect breeding ground for the mosquito. Make sure you bring plenty of repellant, as the swarms can become large enough to bleed you dry in a matter of hours.

Animals

While animal attacks are rare, they do happen. The Uintas have Black Bears, Mountain Lions, Deer, Elk and Moose. When encountering an animal, be sure to keep your distance. Be carefull not to get in between a mother and her offspring as they can be very protective. Keep your campsite free of food that could tempt a late-night visit from a bear or even worse: raccoons.

The biggest danger you will find from animals is while in your car. Pay attention while driving, especially at night as animals will cross the road at any point. You cannot underestimate the damage a 200-800 pound animal can do to your car if you hit it.

Camping

There are 22 developed pay sites along the Mirror Lake Scenic Byway. Most of these offer clean sites including: running water, toilets, picnic tables, and fire rings. For Holidays and weekends you will need to call **877-444-6777** for reservations and more information. You can also log on to **www.reserveusa.com**. These sites range from $6-$12.00 a night. A few of the sites climbers may be interested in are: Soapstone, Trial Lake, Moosehorn, Mirror Lake and Butterfly Lake.

For those who want to save a little dough, there are over 300 unde-veloped, dispersed (free) campsites. All of these sites are marked with a dispersed campsite sign. Many of these are accessed by dirt roads leading off the highway. Campsites must be more than 200 feet from water sources, trails or other campsites. **There may be fire restrictions in place.** Check with the Forest Service before making a campfire. Bring a stove just in case. Please make sure you practice Leave No Trace ethics.

Wilderness Ethics

You are entering a high altitude ecosystem. There are may fragile plant and animal species that can be easily disturbed by your presence. Please minimize your impacts.
- If you carry it in, carry it back out. This includes powerbar wrappers, finger tape, cigarette butts, etc.
- Stay on designated trails. Please use the same trail when accessing the cliff. Avoid fragile vegetation.
- Human waste. Pack it out or use a cat-hole. If you use a cat-hole, make sure you are at least 200 feet from water sources, campsites, trails or cliffs.
- Check the signs along the road or with the Forest Service to see if there are any fire restrictions. Only use existing fire rings if you do build a fire.
- Keep the noise down. If you want to climb or hike with music, use an i-pod or walkman. As frustrating as your 10th fall on your project might be, keep your temper tantrums to yourself. Remember that in many of the climbing areas there are families hiking, camping or picnicking nearby.
- Do not feed or bother the wildlife.
- Be smart and be safe. Use your head and common sense.

Mountain Safety

Always keep in mind that the mountains can be a dangerous place if unprepared. Here are a few tips to help keep you safe.
- Never travel alone.
- Make sure at lease one person not in your group knows where you are going for the day.
- Carry a compass and map and know how to use them. It can be very easy to get lost in the mountains.
- Make sure you have a rain jacket and an insulating piece in your pack.
- Bring enough water. Lack of water at high elevation can quickly lead to dehydration or altitude sickness.
- Treat or filter any water you get from streams or lakes. Sheep and cattle are grazing all over the Uintas and have contaminated almost

every body of water.

- Keep a small first aid kit in your pack. Include matches and a little food.

Recreation Fee Program

Unfortunately, in today's society, it has become necessary to "pay to play." In summer 1997, the Forest Service began charging fees for "recreational" use of the Mirror Lake Highway area. While this has been a point of contention for many user groups, there is an upside to this. All the fees will stay in the Mirror Lake area to maintain the scenic beauty of the area.

A Day Pass is $3.00, and a weekly pass is $6.00. If you plan on spending a lot of time in the Uintas, the Annual Pass is only $25.

New Route Development

There is a lifetime of rock to climb in the Uintas. Although the characteristics of the rock are similar, each crag varies in its ability to take natural protection. The authors encourage you to try to protect a climb with gear if possible. If you do opt to place a bolt, please try to keep the following in mind.

1. Is the climb worth the effort, time and money to bolt? In other words, will anyone else climb it?
2. Is this climb going to destroy natural vegetation?
3. Are you destroying animal habitat by bolting this?
4. Is this climb visible to other user groups? I.e. hikers, fishermen, picnickers.
5. Is the rock of good quality?

The authors feel strongly that all permanent hardware be camouflaged. You can purchase pre-painted hangers, or using several coats, paint them yourself. This reduces the visual impact of a bolt and hangers. Lead bolts should be 3/8" x 2 1/4" at a minimum. Anchors are usually 3/8" x 3".

Ratings

Although we have tried to ensure that the ratings are consistent through all the areas covered, there is still a lot of inconsistency. Climbs at some of the more popular areas have been rated too soft.

While you will still find some of the ratings the same as in previous guidebooks, we have down rated many of the climbs in the more popular areas. We have taken on this unpopular task for many reasons. One of the reasons is simply to keep consistency in the area. It can be frustrating to "hike " a 5.11 at Ruth Lake, and then get shut down on a 5.10 at another area a few miles down the road. Not only is this bad for the psyche, it can give people a false sense of security that can lead to accidents. Many of these routes are new and have not had many ascents. The ratings on these might not be accurate yet. If you do not like the rating we have given a climb, please do the following. Pull out a bottle of whiteout, cover up the rating we have given, and then, using a black pen, write in your own.

Star Ratings

We have used a three star system to try to help your choice of routes for the day.
No star - worth doing if in the area.
★ - A good route.
★★ - Don't miss it.
★★★ - One of the best in the area.
★★★★★ - Sessions. The best route in the Uintas.

First Ascents

There are three abreviations used in this guide:
F.A. - First ascent
FTA. - First toprope ascent
FFA. - First free ascent. (may have been toproped in the past)

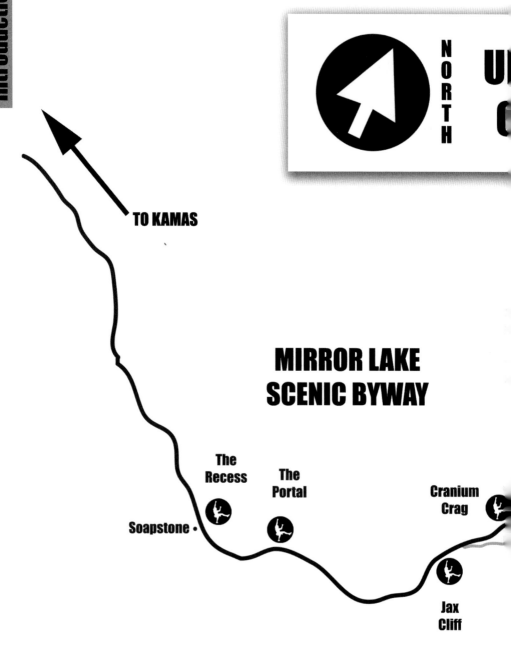

TO KAMAS

N O R T H

**MIRROR LAKE
SCENIC BYWAY**

The
Recess

The
Portal

Soapstone ·

Cranium
Crag

Jax
Cliff

TA ROCK
ERVIEW

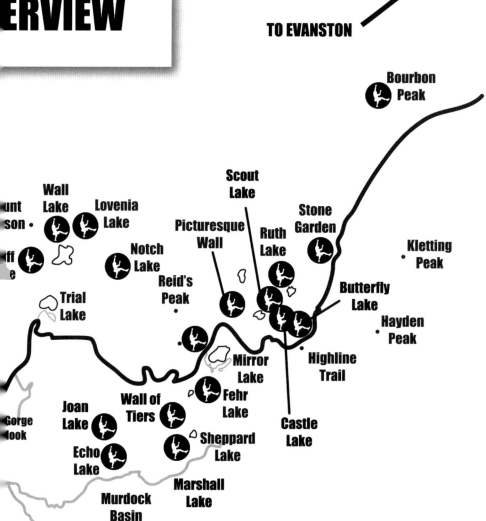

TO EVANSTON

Bourbon
Peak

Scout
Lake

Wall
Lake

Lovenia
Lake

unt
son

ff
e

Notch
Lake

Picturesque
Wall

Ruth
Lake

Stone
Garden

Kletting
Peak

Reid's
Peak

Butterfly
Lake

Hayden
Peak

Trial
Lake

Mirror
Lake

Highline
Trail

Joan
Lake

Wall of
Tiers

Fehr
Lake

Castle
Lake

Gorge
look

Echo
Lake

Sheppard
Lake

Marshall
Lake

Murdock
Basin

25

Uinta Rock

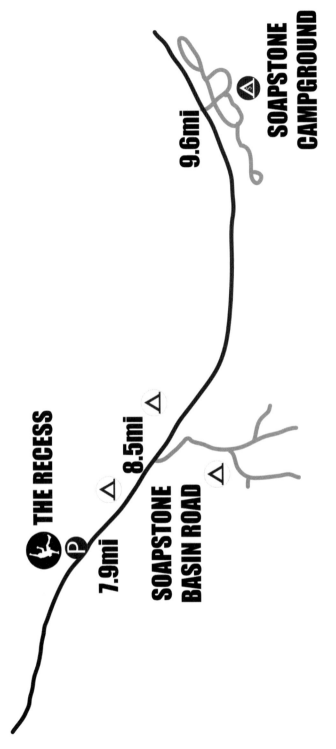

OVERVIEW MAP 1

NORTH

JAX CLIFF

13.7mi

COBBLEREST CAMPGROUND

12.7mi

THE PORTAL

11.9mi

SPRING CANYON RD.

The Recess

Description: The first climbing area encountered on the Mirror Lake Highway. Hidden from view, The Recess offers a secluded traditional climbing experience. Setting up an anchor at the Recess requires a good technical knowledge of gear placement as there are not many trees or boulders to sling. You might have to set up a body belay at the top without protection. There are no bolts here, please keep it this way. All routes developed by either Jonny Woodward or Stuart Ruckman

Directions: Just after mile marker 14 or 7.9 miles from the toll booth and just before Soapstone Basin, pull of on the South side of the road. Cross the road and head up the hill to the obvious notch in the cliff wall. Stay to the right of the talus field, aiming for the large pine on top of a 10 foot cliff. Once you reach this tree, you will see a large cairn to the right. Head to this cairn, then follow the trail back left into the opening. This hike will take about 10 to 15 min. Head through the notch and into The Recess.
USGS Map: Soapstone Basin

Routes described from left to right.

1. Family Duty (VS 4c) 5.8 ★★
25 feet. Start beneath a small roof just left of the dead tree. Good face holds to a crack.
F. A. Jonny Woodward, Stuart Ruckman

2. Ups and Downs (VD 3b) 5.5 ★
30 feet. Start in a corner with good jugs and pro. This route is one of the two downclimbs for this side of the wall.
F.A. Jonny Woodward, Stuart Ruckman

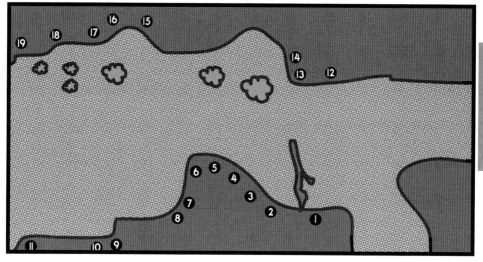

The Recess

3. Top Notch (HS 4b) 5.7 PG ★
30 feet. Start 6 feet right of the corner. Thin face climbing.
F. A. Jonny Woodward, Stuart Ruckman

4. Climax Wall (HS 4b) 5.7 PG ★
30 feet. Start 4-5 feet right of Top Notch. Similar to Top Notch.
F. A. Jonny Woodward, Stuart Ruckman

5. Crash Pad (5a/c) 5.11a
45 feet. The right-most route before the arete. Use thin holds and climb the arete.
F. A. Jonny Woodward, Stuart Ruckman

6. Crash Test (E3 5c) 5.11b R
45 feet. Climb the arete. Thin moves with bad to no gear.
F. A. Jonny Woodward, Stuart Ruckman

7. Un-named 5.10a ★
45 feet. Start on # 8 then go right towards the roof. Big jugs and long pulls await those who pull the roof.
F. A. Jonny Woodward, Stuart Ruckman

8. (HS 4b) 5.7 ★
45 feet. Start in the corner just right of the prow. Easy climbing to an intimidating bulge at the top. Aim straight through the notch at the top of the wall.
F. A. Jonny Woodward, Stuart Ruckman

9. Rocker (S 4a) 5.7- ★
40 feet. Start in a corner 10 feet right of #8. Ok climbing to a good finger crack above a small roof.
F. A. Jonny Woodward, Stuart Ruckman

10. (VS 4b) 5.7 R
40 feet. Same start as Rocker, then go right at the roof following a left-trending feature.
F. A. Jonny Woodward, Stuart Ruckman

11. (S 3c) 5.6 PG
Easy face to two large ledges, then a short headwall with no pro.
F. A. Jonny Woodward, Stuart Ruckman

12. (VS 4c) 5.8-
35 feet.
F. A. Jonny Woodward, Stuart Ruckman

13. (VS 4c) 5.8-
35 feet.
F. A. Jonny Woodward, Stuart Ruckman

14. New Style (HVS 4c) 5.9 R
35 feet. Head straight up the center of the beautifully streaked face.
F. A. Jonny Woodward, Stuart Ruckman

15. Rising Damp (HS 4a) 5.7
35 feet. Start in the indent in the wall. Stay in the left-facing corner system.
F. A. Jonny Woodward, Stuart Ruckman

16. (S 3c) 5.6
35 feet. Start 2 feet left of Rising Damp. Climb the right-facing corner system.
F. A. Jonny Woodward, Stuart Ruckman

17. Blackboard (E2 5b) 5.10d R ★
40 feet. Start behind an aspen. Head up the beautiful black face to an amazingly featured finish. Bad Pro.
F. A. Jonny Woodward, Stuart Ruckman

18. Grim Reachy (E1 5c) 5.11a ★
40 feet. Start with another aspen almost touching your back. Very thin.
F. A. Jonny Woodward, Stuart Ruckman

19. (VS 4c) 5.7+
40 feet. Loose and blocky corner. Starts 6 feet left of Grim Reachy.
F. A. Jonny Woodward, Stuart Ruckman

The Portal

Description: Running for a quarter mile, the Portal wall offers a great traditional experience. The majority of the climbs are 40 feet tall and mostly vertical. There are not many bolts, and many of the trad lines require an expert knowledge in placing and equalizing gear. Topouts can be very sketchy. Often you will have to sit behind a small boulder or bush and belay without any pro. There is also a bit of a bolting war going on between a couple parties. Don't count on the bolts indicated being there when you climb.

Directions: Just after mile marker 18 or mile 11.9 from the toll booth, there are numerous pullouts on either side of the road for the Portal Wall. Head up the talus slope to the route of your choosing. The approach takes about 10 minutes to the base of the wall. USGS Map: Iron Mine Mountain

Routes described from Left to Right:

Not on topo:
Spanish Love 5.11b
Just left of Portal Arete. Toprope.
F.A. Chris Harmston

1. Portal Arete (E1 5a/b) 5.10a
Start just left of the arete and angle right. Follow the arete for a bit then go back left. There are old bolts on the top of this climb, so it might have had an earlier lead.
F.A. Chris Harmston

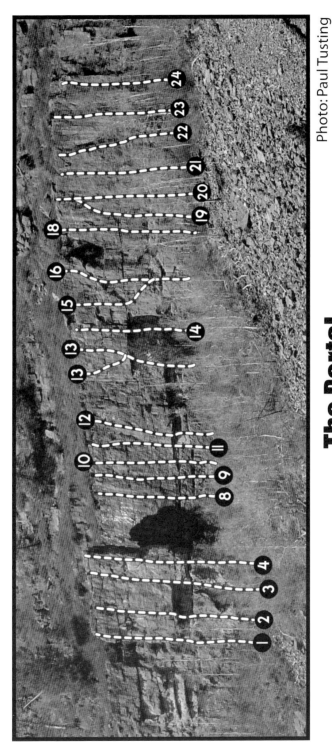

Photo: Paul Tusting

The Portal

The Portal

2. Pillar of Society (E2 5c) 5.10c
Climb the face of the detached pillar on the left side
F.A. Jonny Woodward

3. (E3 5c) 5.10d R
Start in a left-facing corner then pull the crack in the roof.
F.A. Chris Harmston

4. Doggy Pillar (HVS 4c) 5.9 R
Climb the arete.
F.A. Jonny Woodward

5. (VS 4b) 5.7 R
Just right of the arete.
F.A. Jonny Woodward

6. Not Tonight Josephine (E3 5c) 5.10d R
Just right of the arete next to the chimney.
F.A. Jose Pererya

7. (VS 4c) 5.8 PG
Face
F.A. Jonny Woodward

8. (HVS 5a) 5.10a
Thin face that's often wet early season.
F.A. Jonny Woodward

9. (VS 4c) 5.8 PG
Thin face that's often wet early season.
F.A. Jonny Woodward

10. (HVS 5a) 5.10a
Thin face that's often wet early season.
F.A. Jonny Woodward

11. (HS 4b) 5.7
Thin face that's often wet early season.
F.A. Jonny Woodward

12. (VS 4b) 5.7 R
Pull the roof then easier face climbing.
F.A. Jonny Woodward

13. Chopper (E3 5c) 5.10d R
After you pull the roof you have two variations you can use to finish.
The line to the left is the better line, but the right path is easier.
F.A. Jonny Woodward

14. Protraction (HVS 5b) 5.10a
Start in a left-facing corner then pull the crack in the roof.
F.A. Jonny Woodward

15. Son of Elmer (HVS 5a) 5.10a
Go up then left.
F.A. Jonny Woodward

16. Elmer (VS 4c) 5.8 PG
Same start as Son of Elmer then straight up.
F.A. Jonny Woodward

17. Vegetated Cracks (S 4a) 5.6+
F.A. Jonny Woodward

18. Forced Entry (E1 5a) 5.9+ X
F.A. Kennen Harvey

19. No More Mister Fat Guy (E1 5a) 5.9+ X
Up then right to #20's anchors.
F.A. Jonny Woodward

20. 5.10+ X
F.A. Chris Harmston

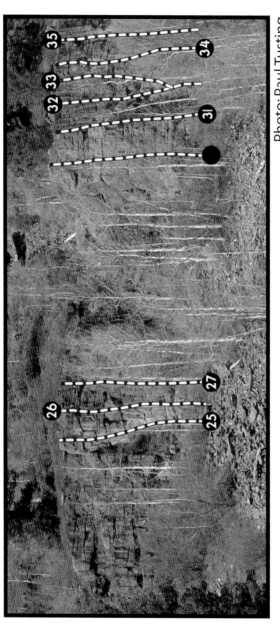

Photo: Paul Tusting

21. Trekkin (E2 5b) 5.10c R
F.A. Jonny Woodward

22. Erie Canal (HVS 4c) 5.9 R
A right-facing shallow corner that trends left.
F.A. Jonny Woodward

23. (E2 5b) 5.10b R
Straight up the streaked wall.
F.A. Jonny Woodward

24. Mid Day Sun (E2 5c) 5.10c PG
Climb just left of the arete.
F.A. Jonny Woodward

25. Bouncer (HS 4a) 5.7
F.A. Jonny Woodward

26. Yorker (VS 4b) 5.7 R
F.A. Jonny Woodward

27. Full Toss (S 3c) 5.6 PG
F.A. Jonny Woodward

28. (HVD 3b) 5.4+ PG
F.A. Jonny Woodward

29. (HVS 5a) 5.10a
F.A. Jonny Woodward

30. (E4 5b) 5.11a X
F.A. Jonny Woodward

31. Borderline (VS 4c) 5.8 PG
F.A. Jonny Woodward, Stuart Ruckman

32. (E1 5b) 5.10a R
F.A. Jonny Woodward, Stuart Ruckman

33. (VS 4c) 5.8 PG
F.A. Jonny Woodward, Stuart Ruckman

34. How About Those Jerks? (VS 4c) 5.8 PG
F.A. Jonny Woodward, Stuart Ruckman

35. Over and Out (VS 4b) 5.8 R
F.A. Jonny Woodward, Stuart Ruckman

The following climbs do not have a topo.

36. Unknown 1
3 bolts plus anchors. Just left of over and out.
F.A. Unknown

37. Unknown 2
3 bolts plus anchors.
F.A. Unknown

38. Unknown 3
4 bolts plus anchors.
F.A. Unknown

40. (VS 4b) 5.7 R
F.A. Jonny Woodward

41. First Gear (E3 5c) 5.10d R
F.A. Jonny Woodward, Stuart Ruckman

42. Syncro Mess (E4 5c) 5.11a
F.A. Jonny Woodward

Photo on following pages:

Heath Christensen
on Jax in the Box
5.10b

Description: Jax Wall is a short but sweet crag of mostly moderate sport lines with a couple of gear routes thrown in for good measure. The cliff is west-facing so receives good afternoon sun. Elevation: 8,700 ft

Directions: To get to the Jax Cliff, park at mile marker 20 by the blue Forest Service sign or 13.7 miles from the toll booth. Follow the trail to edge of a ravine, move left down a ramp and follow the edge of the river until you find a shallow spot where the ravine ends. Cross the river and hike straight up the bank to flat ground. Head back downstream for 300 yards on a bench, then head up into the main talus field (see area map). Take path of least resistance up talus until you can break left to the cliff. Plan on 25-30 steep minutes from car. Routes described from right to left.
USGS Map: Iron Mine Mountain

1. Black Jax 5.10c
35 feet. Harder than it looks. The first ascentionist found this out the hard way when he tried to do this ground-up with gear.
F.A. Nathan Smith. Summer 2002

2. New Jax City 5.9 ★
35 feet. Climbs a left-facing dihedral. Laybacking, pulls, and a little bit of stemming up a black groove. Totally casual and fun. 3 bolts plus anchors.
F.A. Heath Christenson, Paul Tusting. 9/01/02

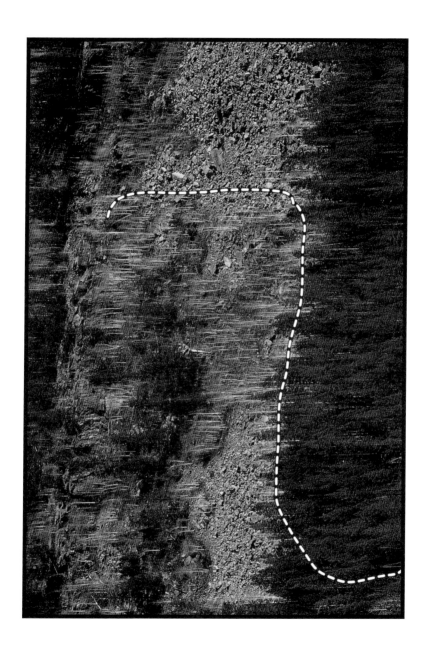

3. Jax in the Box 5.10b ★★

35 feet. A continuous climb with a little kick at the end. 4 bolts plus anchors.

F.A. Paul Tusting, Heath Christenson, Nate Smith. September, 2002

4. Pepper Jax 5.8 ★★

25 feet. Great rock and positive edges lead to a jug at the lip. Top-out and clip the chains. Super fun in-cuts all the way. 3 bolts and anchors.

F.A. Paul Tusting, Heath Christenson. 7/20/02.

5. Jax Rabbit 5.7 ★

30 feet. Hop on up the finger-to-hand crack to a set of chains. Good warm up or first trad lead. Eats any gear you feed it.

F.A. Paul Tusting, Heath Christenson. 7/20/02.

6. Cracker Jax 5.9+

50 feet. Two white boys, two skinny ropes. Climbs face just right of Jax Hammer. Thin gear protects this route well, originally done on half-ropes. Upper face somewhat fractured. Shares anchors with Jax Hammer.

F.A. Paul Tusting, James Loveridge. 10/19/02.

7. Jax Hammer 5.11a ★★

50 feet. Long pulls on good rock with a stout move (or two) in the middle. Free sailing to the top after the crux. 4 bolts plus anchors.

F.A. Heath Christensen, Paul Tusting. 7/20/02.

8. Raspberry Flapjax 5.10c ★

55 feet. Start in the black streak and make a line just right of the raspberry bush halfway up the wall. Longer than it looks. 5 bolts plus anchors.

F.A. Nathan Smith. 8/21/02

9. Roof Jax 5.10+

55 feet. Climbs straight through the large roof left of Raspberry Flapjax and shares the same anchors. A hidden horizontal slot in the headwall above the roof saves the day. Tricky gear to anchors.

F.A. James Loveridge, Paul Tusting. 10/19/02.

Photos: Paul Tusting

Photo on following page:

Paul Tusting on the 1st ascent of Jax in the Box 5.10b

Salt
Lake
Climbers
Alliance

The
SLCA
exists to
promote
climbing
opportunities,
preserve local
access,
and encourage
stewardship of
the environment

www.saltlakeclimbers.org

Cranium Crag

Cranium Crag

Description: The Cranium Crag contains climbs from 40 to 60 ft, protected mostly with gear but often a bolt or two at the start. The crag has a east-facing wall, which receives good morning sun, and south- facing wall that sits in the shade from the trees. Elevation: 9,400 ft

Directions: The Cranium Crag is located across from the Slate Gorge parking area just after mile marker 22 or 16.1 miles from the toll booth. From the parking lot, cross the street and head up towards the obvious cube-shaped cliff above. Once in the lowest talus field, aim for the gully on the right that has a pillar-like formation at the top. Once your reach this point, traverse the ledge system left (south) for 100 yards to the base of the wall. Plan on 20-25 minutes for the approach, which is quick but steep. Routes described from right to left.
USGS Map: Mirror Lake

1. Cranium Crack 5.8+ ★
35 Feet. Climb the steep hand crack just right of the obvious arete using jugs and sinker jams. Mostly hand-sized gear, with a #4 Camalot helpful up high. Gear to anchors.
F.A. Paul Tusting, Chris Harmston. June 9, 2002

2. All There 5.10- ★
40 Feet. Climb the face just left of the arete. Route starts by clipping a bolt behind an aspen then follow horizontals up to the anchors. Small cams are helpful.
F.A. Paul Tusting, James Loveridge. October 12, 2002

3. Badger Me 5.10b

40 feet. Climb through a small roof and up the black streak in the center of the face. Two bolts then gear. Angle right to anchors on the route above. Use caution until first bolt is clipped.
F.A. Chris Harmston, Paul Tusting. June 9, 2002

4. Tree Hugger 5.11b

50 feet. Start below large ominous roofs left of obvious steep prow. Climb slab up into the corner. Traverse out horizontal crack to jug at lip. Follow patina face to top. No anchors, walk off to the left.
F.A. project

5. Brain Stem 5.10- ★

40 Feet. One good tug through roof then basic reflexes will take you to the top. Two bolts plus to gear to the anchors. Plug in gear below roof if needed, but watch for rope drag.
F.A. Paul Tusting, Chris Harmston. June 9, 2002

Uinta Rock

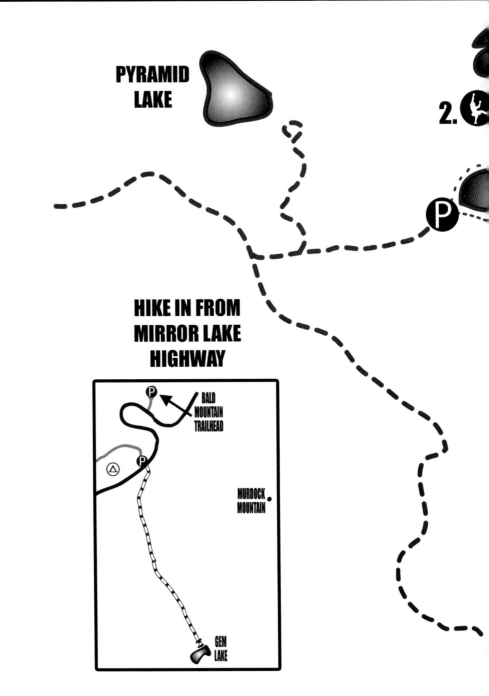

PYRAMID
LAKE

2.

P

HIKE IN FROM
MIRROR LAKE
HIGHWAY

P ← BALD
MOUNTAIN
TRAILHEAD

P

MURDOCK
MOUNTAIN

GEM
LAKE

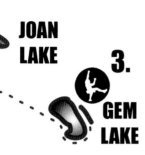

JOAN LAKE

3.

GEM LAKE

ECHO LAKE

1.

MURDOCK BASIN

NORTH

1. ECHO LAKE
2. JOAN LAKE
3. GEM LAKE
4. MARSHALL LAKE

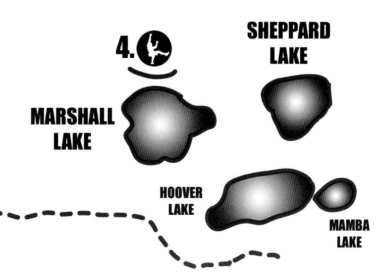

4.

SHEPPARD LAKE

MARSHALL LAKE

HOOVER LAKE

MAMBA LAKE

Murdock Basin

Description: Murdock Basin is filled with small cliffs and not much fixed protection. The exception to this is the Comeposer Wall which is quite tall (some routes require two-rope rappels) and has some lead bolts and anchor stations. There are two ways to get to Murdock Basin. The first is driving up a very rough dirt road. The second is hiking over the saddle between Murdock Mountain and Mount Cardwell from the Mirror Lake Highway, which takes about an hour but is required if you do not have a high clearance vehicle. To climb here you need an exploratory personality and good navigating skills in the backcountry. There is still a lot of new route potential. Elevation: 9,750-10,200 ft

Directions:

From Murdock Road: Take the Murdock Basin turnoff from the Mirror Lake Highway, which is marked with a sign. This is located between mile-marker 21 and 22 or 15.2 miles from the tollbooth, then leads to the right off of route 140 when coming from the Kamas side. If you get to the Slate Gorge Overlook, you have gone too far. Murdock Basin Road remains relatively well-maintained until a fork in the road about 2 miles from the highway. One dirt road heads right and down into the north fork of the Duchesne River. Follow the left fork which gets progressively worse. About three miles later take the obvious left turn. If you miss this turn you will immediately run into a small creek crossing the road and will know you went too far. The road you turned left onto will get worse, but will take you to Pyramid Lake (next left) and Echo Lake (stay straight). Park at Echo Lake. This last section is about a mile long and is full-on 4X4.

From Bald Mountain Pass: Park at a dirt turnoff on the west-side of the road 22.5 miles from the tollbooth or .2 miles before Bald Mountain Overlook. Cross the road and head up a small but steep drainage. Keep moving right and uphill to the saddle and a huge flat talus field, which gives the first look into Murdock Basin. You should be able to see the blunt summit of Mount Cardwell and Blizzard Lake to your right on the Murdock Basin side of the saddle. The other lakes will be hard to see as they are on lower benches. Head downhill in a southeast direction until either Joan or Gem Lake come into view. The hike into Murdock Basin is easier than the hike out, so save some energy. See the overview map and approach descriptions to individual cliffs for more info.

USGS Map: Mirror Lake

Echo Lake - Comeposer Wall

The Comeposer Wall is quite steep and long. The routes from the main cliff will require two ropes to descend, but all are single-pitch routes up to 130 ft in length.

Directions:

Follow the directions above to Echo Lake. From where the dirt road ends, head right around the lake following its eastern shore. The cliff is located at the opposite end of the lake from the parking and should only take about 10-15 minutes to reach from your jeep. If you find yourself on the western shore of the lake when hiking in from the Mirror Lake Highway, just follow the shore around to the northeast corner where the cliff is located. The western shore is much rougher to follow than the path on the eastern side. Routes described left to right.

1. Dragon's Tooth 5.10

This route is located about 100 yards left of the main wall. It involves climbing up a slab on a detached pillar then traversing left into a steep corner using a big horizontal. Watch out to not dislodge the "dragon's tooth" as you pass by. Climb the steep hand crack, exit out right, and set a gear belay. Walk off to the right.

F.A. Paul Tusting, Chris Harmston. Summer 2000.

Uinta Rock

Dragon's Tooth

Photo: Paul Tusting

2. Low Route 5.7
This is the left-most route of the main wall. Scramble up onto a big ledge then rope up and climb a fractured slab to a tree with slings. Shorter and easier than the other routes at the crag.
F.A. Paul Tusting, Marie Midbow. Summer 2000.

3. Chosstakovich 5.10b ★★
Face to the right of the Low Route pillar. High quality rock and climbing on gear to a set of anchors.
F.A. Chris Harmston, Marie Midbow, Paul Tusting. Summer 2000.

4. Rockmungenough 5.11a/b
Climb the double hand cracks on the right side of the wide chimney through a thin roof then up a large steep dihedral. Exit the dihedral to right and climb up to a set of anchors.
F.A. Chris Harmston. Summer 2000.

5. A Song and Dance 5.11+ b/c
Climb Rockmungenough or Pro Coffee Yes to the start of the dihedral, then move right over the large roof. Climb the overhanging arete to the same anchors.
F.A. Doug Heinrich, Chris Harmston. Summer 2000.

6. Pro Coffee Yes 5.11d ★★
Climbing a thin face and seams past two bolts then exit up the left corner avoiding the large block. Cross Rockmungenough and exit the dihedral to the left which leads to a set of anchors.
F.A. Chris Harmston, Doug Heinrich. 9/13/01

Comeposer Wall

7. Harmony 5.10d ★★★

Climb the prominent prow starting with a handcrack then move onto the steep nose and climb big horizontals. Best route on the wall. Gear (tcu's) to anchors. 2 rope rappel

F.A. Chris Harmston. Summer 2000.

8. Dischord 5.10d
Follow Harmony to just below the final steep arete section. Move right and climb up the face about 15ft right of the prow. At the top, traverse back to the anchors on Harmony.
F.A. Chris Harmston. Summer 2000.

9. Black Rapshoddy 5.10a ★★★
Climb the flake splitting the roof on the right-side of the cliff, about 10 ft from the prow. Once on the ledge about halfway up, follow the steep black face up to a tree belay.
F.A. Paul Tusting, Chris Harmston. Summer 2000.

10. Dead Comeposer's Society 5.10d R
Climb through the roof about 10ft right of Black Rapshoddy then finish either on Black Rapshoddy or Harmony. Watch out for bad rock and really bad pro. Not recommended.
F.A. Chris Harmston, Marie Midbow. Summer 2000.

11. Tone Deaf 5.9+
Bypass all of the roofs on the eastern face of the Echo Lake wall by flanking them to the right. Starts just left an obvious wide crack. Once on the midway ledge system, head up the face to the right of Black Rapshoddy to a tree. Watch out for loose rock.
F.A. Chris Harmston. Summer 2001.

12. The Dead Tree Dance 5.9
Slightly right of the main crag on a shorter section. Follow steep finger crack to a dead tree. Then dance!
F.A. Brian Cabe, Randy Klimes. 7/04/01

Twin Peaks and Big Momma Areas
Description: The Twin Peaks are a small and moderate trad area just below Joan Lake. There are no fixed anchors, but there is some potential for harder routes requiring fixed pro on the Right Peak.
Directions:
From the Echo Lake Parking area, follow the left shore of the lake around until you reach a gully with a steam. The left side of the gully has a short cliff. Hike up the gully for 5-10 minutes until Left Peak

Photo: Paul Tusting

Comeposer Wall

becomes visible to your right. When hiking in from the Mirror Lake
Highway, find a small stream exiting Joan Lake on the east-side and
follow it down to the crags.

Uinto Rock

Photo: Paul Tusting

Left Peak

Left Peak

Routes described left to right and are up to 60 ft in length.

1. Gary's Prow 5.5
Climb up right side of arete placing gear in the horizontals. Belay in trees and walk off.
F.A. Gary Barnett, Paul Tusting. Summer 2000.

2. Eager Beaver 5.9 R
Climb slab through roof keeping off the mini arete on left. Climb though loose blocks to top. TCU's and small nuts are useful. Belay in trees and walk off. Contrived.
F.A. Paul Tusting, Mark Allgood. Summer 2000.

3. Mark's Slab 5.8
Climb slab right of Eager Beaver to top. Belay in trees and walk off.
F.A. Mark Allgood, Paul Tusting. Summer 2000.

Murdock Basin

4. Shitty Bulge 5.9

Not recommended. Climb straight up steep bulge on short right-end of cliff. Belay in trees and walk off.

F.A. Paul Tusting, Mark Allgood. Summer 2000.

Right Peak

Photo: Paul Tusting

Right Peak

Just 50 ft north of Left Peak and a little steeper.

1. Dirty Girl 5.9+ ★

Start up thin crack in left-most part of cliff. Climb to the ledge system, and traverse to right. Climb steep hand crack through head wall. Belay in trees and walk off.

F.A. Paul Tusting, Gary Barnett. Summer 2000.

Big Momma Area

The Big Momma Area is even shorter than the Twin Peaks and is only worth visiting if in the area. A discontinuous cliff bridges the benches that contain Twin Peaks and Joan Lake. From Twin Peaks, follow the cliff system north for a couple hundred yards to the Big Momma roof.

1. Big Momma 5.11- ★

Climb the cleft splitting the roof about 10 ft off the ground. Place thin cams and nuts and move left and up to the top of the cliff. Belay in the trees and walk off. There is an uncompleted 5.8 hand crack on the corner of the formation.

F.A. Paul Tusting, Gary Barnett. Summer 2000.

2. Easy Slab 5.7 (no photo or topo)
Located 100 ft right of the Big Momma and faces north. Gear to a tree belay and a walk off. F.A. Paul Tusting, Gary Barnett. Summer 2000.

Big Momma Wall

Gem Lake

Directions: Likely you will come upon Gem Lake as you descend from the saddle between Murdock Mountain and Mount Cardwell. It is a small lake, shaped like a peanut. Right on the northwest edge of the lake is an unclimbed slab, and if you head uphill following a small stream for about 200, yards you will come upon more unclimbed slabs and a steep wall. The routes below are on the steep wall, which has no fixed anchors. From Echo Lake parking, follow the directions to Twin Peaks and Joan Lake, then head north on a large bench to find Gem Lake. Routes described left to right.

1. Much Ado About Nothing 5.8
Ok at best. Follow the steep hand crack on the left edge of a dihedral on the cliff's left side up and around to a slab. Walk off.
F.A. Paul Tusting, Mike McBride. 8/12/03.

Gem Lake

2. Mid Day Lighting 5.10+ ★★

Quite good. Climb a seam up through a roof to access a steep right facing corner system. Follow this up and either set a belay in horizontal cracks or up in the trees and walk off.

F.A. James Loveridge, Trent Baker, Paul Tusting, Mike McBride. 8/12/03.

3. Mid-day Lighting Direct 5.11+

Direct top-rope from the end of Mid-day Lighting. Would make a fine sport route.

F.A. Trent Baker. 8/12/03.

4. Trent's Roof 5.10+

Climb a corner system to access a large steep roof. A heel-hook saves the day as you exit the roof. Belay in the trees and walk off.

F.A. Trent Baker, James Loveridge. 8/12/03.

Uinta Rock

Marshall Lake Cliff

Description: Marshall Lake is a very large cliff which faces east and has a top tier which is similar to Ruth Lake but requires about 200 ft of scrambling to access. There is a lot of route potential in this area.

Directions:

To get to Marshall Lake either follow the Murdock Basin Road past the turnoff for Echo Lake (cross the stream described in the directions above) until the large cliff become visible at which point a turnoff to the left leads to the lake, or hike in from the Fehr Lake trailhead. This is a long hike which looses significant elevation. Something to consider after a long tiresome day of climbing.

1. A Long Trip for a Great View 5.10a R

Approach this route on the left side of the cliff. Scramble up about 200 ft to a 5.7 corner system that deposits you on the ledge below the route. What you are headed for is the very clean upper band of the cliff. This route ascends a crack up the largest and widest face in this tier. You reach the crack via a 5.10 traverse from the right with tricky gear. The crack is 5.8 and quite good. One 60m rope will get you from the anchors to the ledge system where there is a rap station. Use two 60m ropes from this anchor and scramble back down to the base.

F.A. Paul Tusting, Todd Berlier. Summer 2001

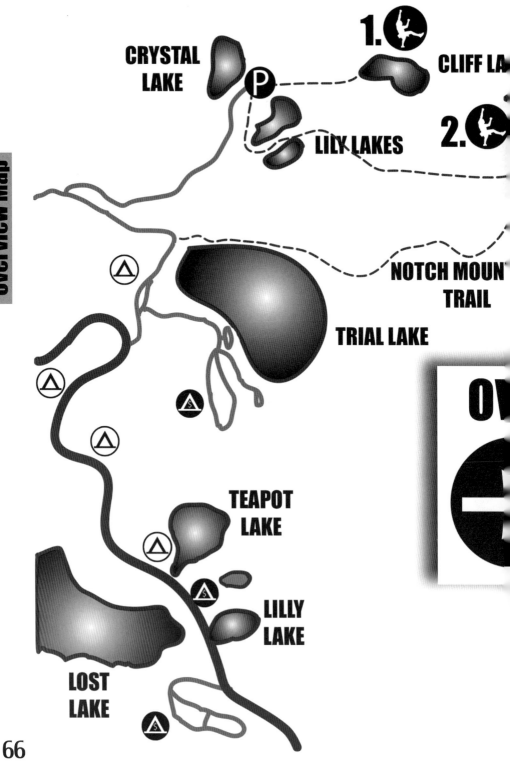

CRYSTAL LAKE

1.

CLIFF LA

2.

LILY LAKES

NOTCH MOUN
TRAIL

TRIAL LAKE

OV

TEAPOT LAKE

LILLY LAKE

LOST LAKE

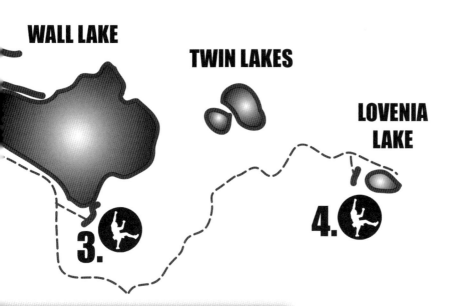

WALL LAKE

TWIN LAKES

LOVENIA LAKE

RVIEW MAP 3

N O R T H

1. CLIFF LAKE
2. WALL LAKE
3. SCARY SPICE
4. LOVENIA LAKE

Notch Lake

Wall Lake

Wall Lake

Lake

Description: Wall Lake is surrounded by a group of small cliffs varying is height from 20 ft to 80 ft. Most of the cliffs have large trees above them, as well as easy access to the top. Due to this and the popularity of hiking in the area, fixed hardware has been minimized. Some routes have top rope anchors below the lip but don't rely on finding these, as they may be hard to reach. Bring at least a 30 ft section of webbing or static rope to set top anchors. Most of the routes are moderate, and only a few have names and descriptions. Use your imagination and keep an eye out for loose rock. This is a great place for summer picnics. The different cliffs vary in exposure. White Pine in Park City often uses these cliffs for guiding. If you come upon one of their groups, please respect that this is how they make a living.
Elevation: 10,200 ft.

Directions: Park at the Trial Lake parking area then hike north on the trail heading for Wall Lake and Notch Mountain. Follow the relatively flat and obvious trail one mile north to Wall Lake.
USGS Map: Mirror Lake

Wall Lake Cliff
This is the obvious discontinuous cliff on the eastern shore of the lake.
There are several top ropes on the south facing side in the 5.6 range.

Wall Lake

Wall Lake Slab

Parallel to the Wall Lake Cliff but set behind it by several hundred yards. This cliff is approximately 80 ft high and 500 ft long. It is mostly low angled with some bulges on the left end. Watch the tails of your ropes when lowering.

Many moderate top-ropes exist on this cliff in the 5.6-5.9 range.

Uinta Rock

The Scary Spice Wall

Description: This series of cliff bands is shorter than the other walls at Wall Lake but higher quality and has more difficult routes. There are plenty of trees at the top of the cliff to top-rope from if you want to, or you can lead the routes with gear. There are no fixed anchors.

Directions: From the main trail on the southeast end of Wall Lake, continue along the trail on the right side of the lake towards Notch Mountain. In about 1/4 mile there will be a fork in the trail. Take the left and more faint trail. You will drop down into a creek bed then head uphill. Within 100 yds you will come to the Scary Spice Buttress.

Routes are described right to left.

1. Rad Meets Sad 5.7
30 ft. Climb the slab just right of the boulder at the base of the wall. Reasonable gear takes you to the top. Belay from trees.
F.A. Paul Tusting, Joey D'Achino. Summer 2001.

2. Scary Spice 5.11- R ★
30 ft. Climb through the steep horizontals directed above the boulder at the base of the wall. Small nuts and cams helpful, or use a top-rope.
F.A. Paul Tusting, Joey D'Achino. Summer 2001.

3. Inside Scoop 5.9
30 ft. This route climbs the inside corner to the left of Scary Spice. Pull a bulge to start, then cruse up on gear.
F.A. Paul Tusting, Joey D'Achino. Summer 2001.

4. TR Prow 5.10 ★
Climb the clean prow just right of Inside Scoop. A top-rope problem as no natural gear is available.
F.A. Paul Tusting, Joey D'Achino. Summer 2001.

Scary Spice Wall

5. Why Not 5.9 R

Not a particularly enjoyable lead. Climb the subtle groove on the left edge of the cliff next to the clean prow described above.
F.A. Paul Tusting, Joey D'Achino. Summer 2001.

Cliff Lake

Cliff Lake

Cliff Lake

Description: Cliff Lake is a serene lake sitting above the valley floor. All routes are 60 to 90 feet in length. Make sure you bring a rack, as even the sport lines can use supplemental gear.
Elevation: 10,362 ft.

Directions: From the Trial Lake parking area, head east on the trail heading for Long and Island Lakes. Within a half mile there will be a smaller trail (with a small metal sign stating: Cliff Lake) heading off to the right towards Cliff Lake. Follow this up-hill to the lake. Once at the lake go left to the obvious cliff. Approach will take 20-30 minutes.
USGS Map: Mirror Lake

From left to right

1. Mosquito Mayhem 5.7 (Not on topo)
This climb is just left of the cliff-band shown in the photo. Traverse the low angle slab to a steep face. All trad, no anchor.
F.A. Brian Cabe, Patricia Black. 6/29/02

2. Squanto 5.10 ★★
6 bolts, 1 fixed piton, to bolted anchor.
F.A. Brian Smoot, Brian Cabe. 6/27/02

3. Chilly Dogs 5.10 ★
Shares anchors with #2. 8 bolts to bolted anchor.
F.A. Brian Smoot, Brian Cabe. 6/27/02

Cliff Lake

4. No Woman, No Cry 5.10c ★★

8 bolts to bolted anchor. Several variations for start and middle.
F.A. Brian Cabe, Matt Scullian, Dwight Curry. 8/4/03

5. Butter Face 5.5

Worth doing if in the area.
F.A. Brian Cabe (solo). 6/29/02

6. Glory (A.K.A. What Price for Glory?) 5.7 ★★
8 bolts to bolted anchor.
F.A. Brian Cabe. 6/26/02

7. Vulgaria (A.K.A. A Pox in Vulgaria) 5.8 ★★★
8 bolts to bolted anchor.
F.A. Brian Cabe, Brian Smoot. 6/27/02

8. Lake Effect 5.9 ★★
Gear to a single bolt above the second small roof. Bolted anchor.
F.A. Brian Cabe, Patricia Black. 8/24/02

9. Gobslutch 5.9 ★
Climb the right hand roof crack into #8. Gear: one bolt to a bolted anchor.
F.A. Brian Cabe, Patricia Black. 8/24/02

Rip Griffith on The Legend, 5.10c, Ruth Lake
Photo: Chris Harmston

Lovenia Lake
Lovenia Lake

A.K.A. The Notch

Description: Lovenia Lake is located in the pass of Notch Mountain. The routes ascend the 70 ft slab facing north just above the lake. There is no fixed gear on this cliff due to its proximity to the hiking trail and Jonny being a "raised-on-gritstone" Brit. Mostly thin edge and crack climbing above thin protection. Top roping is possible but creativity will be needed to find solid belays. Overall the rock quality is good. The day this cliff was developed a mist and threatening clouds hung in the notch reminiscing of a good day in the Peak District. Half ropes could be helpful.
Elevation: 10,700 ft.

Directions: Follow the same directions as for Wall Lake then keep on the trail as it follows the right-hand side of the lake and up some switchbacks to a pass which is approximately 1 mile past Wall Lake. Just as the trail starts steeply descending towards Ibantik Lake you will see the cliff on the right side of the trail. Routes described left to right.
USGS Map: Mirror Lake

1. Just Keep Reaching 5.9+ R ★
60 ft. Pull through the bulge on the left corner of the cliff. Follow the face to the ledge above, and climb through a little bit of looseness to top. No anchors.
F.A. Paul Tusting, Jonny Woodward. Summer 2001

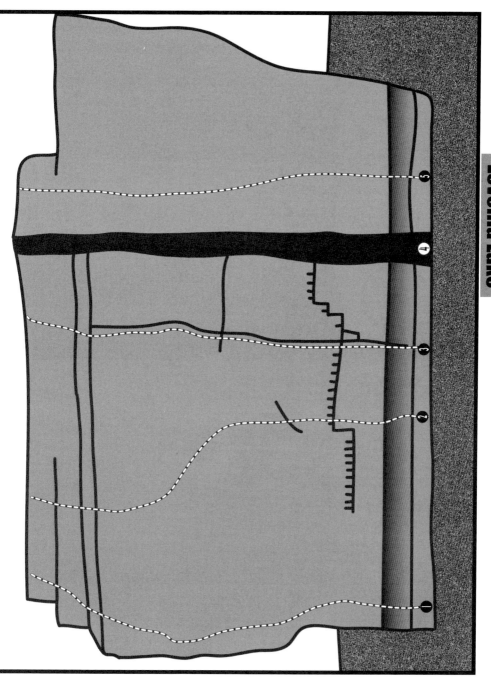

Lovenia Lake

2. No Wonder Brits Have Crooked Teeth 5.10+ R/X ★★
70 ft. If you are into edge climbing way above dubious gear, then this is the route for you. Pass through a couple small roofs, place some small pro in a horizontal and punch it to a ledge. Breath, then finish the last 20 easy feet to the top. No anchors.
F.A. Paul Tusting, Jonny Woodward. Summer 2001

3. Jesus Shoes on the Approach 5.8 ★
70 ft. Follow the finger crack to the left of Big Bertha. Straight forward and easier to protect than the harder routes. No anchors.
F.A. Jonny Woodward, Paul Tusting. Summer 2001

4. Big Bertha 5.7
60 ft. Climb a wide crack in the face. Not particularly clean or enjoyable. No anchors.
F.A. Paul Tusting, Jonny Woodward. Summer 2001

5. HVS 5.9+ R
50 ft. Climb seams to the right of the obvious wide crack. Bring thin gear. No anchors.
F.A. Jonny Woodward, Paul Tusting. Summer 2001

Kathy Harmston on Indian Summer, 5.10a, Ruth Lake
Photo: Chris Harmston

Notch Lake

Notch Lake

The Getaway Wall at Notch Lake

Description: The Getaway Wall is host to a good day or two's worth of climbing. The majority of the climbs weigh in around 5.10+ to 5.11+ but there is much potential for easier routes. Many of the routes here are slightly overhanging.
Elevation: 10,300' feet.

Directions: Start at the Bald Mountain trailhead 23 miles from the toll booth or just after mile marker 29, and head west on the trail for 2.3 miles to Notch Lake. You will have a gentle descent down to the lake losing 500 feet of elevation. Remember this as you find the return a little more strenuous than you expected. This is a well-maintained trail that gets a lot of backpacking traffic. Once you reach the lake, head south along the shore to the cliffs. With a light pack, you can expect this approach to take 30 to 45 min. There is great camping around the lake, with springs for water on the west side of the lake. This cliff faces east and is in the shade by 1:00pm.
USGS Map: Mirror Lake

Routes described from left to right.

1. Secret Knowledge Overkill 5.9
25 feet. Starts up the center of the prominent bulge and stays left of the roof. All Gear. Sling the tree for an anchor.
F.A. John Rogers, Spike Cotter, Greg Kirchoff. Summer 2003

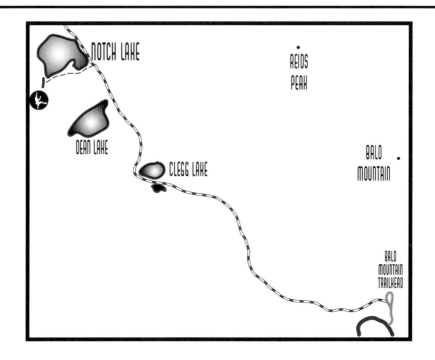

KEVIN C. ROGERS 2004

2. Sport Rappelling is Neither 5.9 ★

55 feet. Starts on the left edge of the Getaway Wall and angles rightwards to Neophyte's anchors. The day this was bolted, the cliff was invaded by 20 sport rappelers. 5 bolts to anchors.
F.A. Nathan Smith. Summer 2002

3. Neophyte 5.10b ★★

60 feet. A small roof then many bulges on a slightly overhanging face. 7 bolts to anchors.
F.A. Heath Christenson, Nathan Smith. Fall 2001

4. Wine of Purity 5.11a ★★★

70 feet. Pull the roof and then try not to pump out on the face. Be prepared to log some airtime at the top. 8 bolts to anchors.
F.A. Nathan Smith. Fall 2001

5. Vinegar of Hostility 5.11d ★★

70 feet. A powerful crux at the start leads to a second crux on the upper headwall. The start is a little reminiscent of Rifle. Use a stick clip to hang the 3rd draw. 8 bolts to anchors.
F.A. Nathan Smith. 6/22/02

6. Tipping the Vessel of Knowledge 5.11d ★★★

30 feet. A harder version of the Wasatch classic Black Monday. Steep and juggy with long moves. Be prepared to mantle. 4 bolts to anchors.
F.A. Nathan Smith. 6/8/02

7. Prisoner of My Own Subconscious 5.10d ★

Start in a corner and head onto the face. Pull the roof at the top. Harder than it looks.
F.A. John Rogers, Spike Cotter, Greg Kirchoff. Summer 2003

8. Bolt School 5.6

A "Gunks" style climb. All gear to a bolted anchor.
F.A. John Rogers, Spike Cotter, Greg Kirchoff. Summer 2003

Notch Lake

9. Size Matters Not 5.10c ★

40 feet. Long moves and blind reaches makes this a lot harder if you are short. It could be pretty hard for a "vertically challenged" person to place draws on lead. 4 bolts to anchors.
F.A. Nathan Smith, Matt Krise, Paul Tusting. 6/16/02

10. The Bearer of Light 5.11a ★★

35 feet. A harder version of Size Matters Not. Again, harder if you are short. 4 bolts to anchors.
F.A. Nathan Smith, Matt Krise, Paul Tusting. 6/16/02

Nathan Smith on Wine of Purity 5.11a, Notch Lake
Photo: Jeff Baldwin

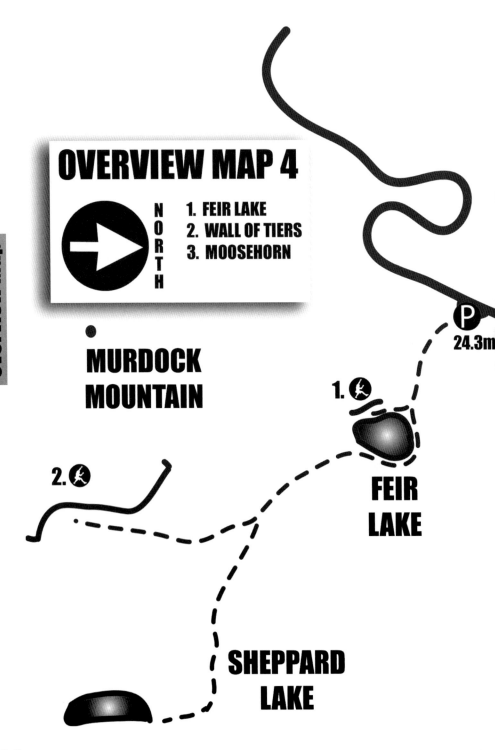

OVERVIEW MAP 4

NORTH

1. FEIR LAKE
2. WALL OF TIERS
3. MOOSEHORN

MURDOCK
MOUNTAIN

P
24.3m

1.

2.

FEIR
LAKE

SHEPPARD
LAKE

Overview Map

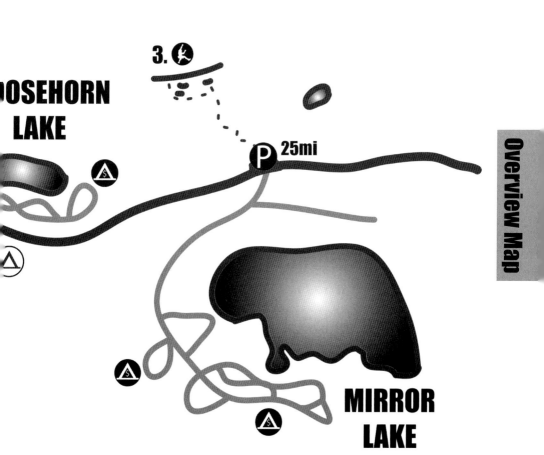

**BALD
MOUNTAIN**

3.

**OSEHORN
LAKE**

P 25mi

**MIRROR
LAKE**

Fehr Lake

Fehr Lake

Description: This wall offers short but steep climbing with the main wall containing good quality rock. Make sure you have a full rack, as these are no sport routes. This wall receives morning sun and is in the shade by noon.
Elevation: 10,260 ft.

Directions: This small crag is set on a small lake hidden just minutes off the road. 24.3 miles from the toll booth, 100 yards south of the Moosehorn Campground you will find a descent parking lot on the east side of the road. A quick and easy .3 mile hike will bring you to this crag. Once you reach the lake, take the lake's shore to the right.
USGS Map: Mirror Lake

Routes described from left to right.

1. Not Fehr Long 5.10d ★
Start on easy crack, then move left out the roof. Finish on the arete.
F.A. Fred Henion

2. Fehr Too Long 5.9 R ★
55 feet. Start a few feet right of #1. Pull the roof then follow the most obvious line of weakness to the top. No anchors.
F.A. Rip Griffith

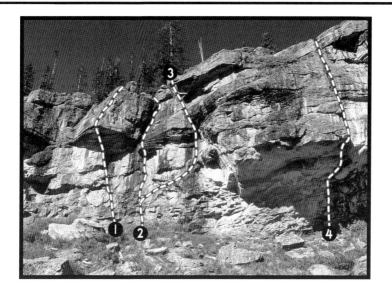

3. Unfehr 5.10b ★★
55 feet. Same start as Fehr Too Long but traverse right and into the corner. No anchors.
F.A. Rip Griffith

4. Fehra Fawcet 5.11d ★★
Roof crack to corner. Watch out for rope drag. Shares anchors with 5.
F.A. Fred Henion

5. Fehr Thee Well 5.11c ★★
Follow the bolt then pull the roof. 2 bolts plus anchors.
F.A. Fred Henion

6. Fehris Buehler 5.11b ★★
Climb a face with one bolt. Pull the roof on the right side. 1 bolt plus anchors.
F.A. Fred Henion

7. All's Fehr 5.11c ★
Shares anchors with 6. Strenuous and tricky gear placements.
F.A. Fred Henion

8. No Fehr 5.10d ★
Pull a low roof and follow a black streak to the top.
F.A. Fred Henion

9. Oh Fehr Rude 5.11a ★
Follow the wide crack through a roof then easy face to the top. Bring a large cam.
F.A. Fred Henion

10. Fehr Game 5.8
55 feet. Climb the corner. No anchor.
F.A. Rip Griffith

11. Currant Affehr 5.8 (Not on topo)
40 feet. Traverse right above the currant bushes then pull a roof.
F.A. Rip Griffith

KEVIN C. ROGERS 2004

Uinto Rock

Wall of Tiers

Wall of Tiers

Description: As the name implies, there are many tiers of rock above the main cliffs. This ads a HIGH DANGER OF ROCKFALL. This fact along with a base full of talus makes this a less then ideal location to bring kids or dogs. The Wall of Tiers is made up of a series of 40-100 ft cliff bands. Most have a east exposure. Although there is some very overhanging terrain these cliffs are filled with 5.8 to 5.11 traditional climbs from just under to just over-vertical. As this guide goes to print, many of these routes have only seen a few ascents. Please take the ratings with a grain of salt.
Elevation: 10,500 ft

Directions: Park at the Fehr Lake parking area and trailhead 24.3 Miles from the tollbooth. This is a large dirt pullout on the east-side of the road across the street from the Moosehorn campground. From here, follow the trail east across several meadows and Fehr Lake. About 1/4 mile past Fehr Lake and about 300 yards past the second large meadow, break off the trail heading south (right) at a cairn (If you start to head downhill on the trail, you have gone too far). The large series of cliffs to the right should just have become visible after you head up a small hill. Follow the bench to the base of the talus field. For the Shield and Attic head straight up from this talus field. For the Far Side, stay at the base of the talus and traverse south until directly below a distinct cliff in the back corner of the cirque. See the overview photo for more info. Plan for 35-45 min for the approach.
USGS Map: Mirror Lake

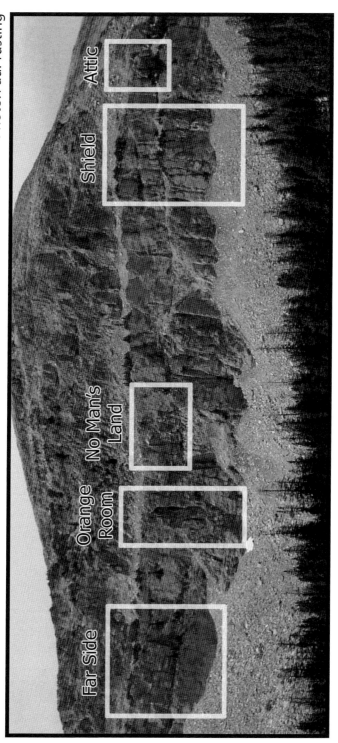

Photo: Paul Tusting

Attic

Shield

No Man's Land

Orange Room

Far Side

Uinta Rock

The Shield

This is the main wall, with a obvious shield like feature on the left side. A single 60m rope will get you off all of these routes.
Routes described from right to left.

1. Retriever 5.10 a/b (No Topo or Photo)

Climb up a loose chimney four feet to the right of Golden. Move left onto the face with an awkward mantle 2/3 of the way up. 2 bolts and gear to the same anchors as Golden. A better variation is to top-rope up the first corner of Golden and then move right onto the face.
F.A. Chris Harmston. Summer 2002.

2. Golden 5.9 ★★★ (No Topo or Photo)

Climbs a shallow left-facing dihedral which then switches directions. Excellent route. Follow this feature to a set of anchors. Gear to anchors.
F.A. Chris Harmston, Tyson Bradley. Summer 2002.

3. The Mace 5.10a ★ (No Topo or Photo)

Climb a face between a south-facing dihedral and a right-slanting northeast facing dihedral, joining the right-slanting dihedral just below mid-height for a bit before going back onto the face. Stay out of the chimney to your right at the top. Loose finish to anchors.
F.A. Rip Griffith, Summer 2002

4. The Halberd 5.10a ★ (No Topo or Photo)

Climb the right-slanting dihedral and finish on the Mace. Watch out for a loose block about halfway up. Shares anchors with the chimney above.
F.A. Rip Griffith, Summer 2002

5. The Thin Thing 5.11 R ★

Climb the short prow split with a seam for 30 ft to a ledge system. Move left out of the chimney onto a face with good horizontals. 5.8 climbing takes you to the chains of the route below. Gear: at least one set of micronuts are mandatory plus a standard rack.
F.A. Project

Wall of Tiers

Wall of Tiers

The Shield

Chris Harmston on Got my Goat 5.11b, The Far Side Photo: Paul Tusting

6. The Thick Thing 5.10a R ★

Stem the corner just left of The Thin Thing. Move right through the roof to the same ledge as described above. From here, follow the path described above. Double set of small cams and single set of large cams are needed. Double ropes and long slings can help rope drag. Otherwise expect serious rope drag.
F.A. Rip Griffith. Summer 2002.

7. Realization 5.11b ★★

Follow a line of five bolts up a layback flake. Face climb right then left on gear to a set of anchors.
F.A. Chris Harmston, Summer 2002

8. Harmful Variants 5.11b

Same start as Realization but moves left following a crack to join Utahpia.
F.A. Chris Harmston, Summer 2003

9. Utahpia 5.11c ★

Climb past three bolts to a ledge. Climb the overhanging corner with solid blocks to another ledge. Climb up a face broken with a splitter crack. 3 bolts then gear to the anchors.
F.A. Chris Harmston, Tyson Bradley. Summer 2002.

10. Utahpia Variation 5.11c

Climb Utahpia to the end of the prominent steep corner about half-way up, then head left across the face to the anchors on Panty Shield.
F.A. Chris Harmston. Summer 2002.

11. Panty Shield 5.11 R ★★★

Climb past two bolts on the right-side of the wall to the left of Utahpia. Continue up face climbing and placing protection past one more bolt to a set of anchors. Very runout start for shorter people.
F.A. Fred Henion. Summer 2001.

12. Stay Free 5.11c R ★★

Climb up a discontinuous crack system to a large roof. Pull the roof and clip a lone bolt. Shares anchors with Panty Shield
F.A. Fred Henion. Summer 2001.

13. Stay Free Variation 5.10 R

Climb Stay Free but skip its crux by heading left below the big roof to the anchors on the 5.10 below.
F.A. Fred Henion. Summer 2001.

14. Soak it Insideher 5.10a ★★★

Climb a crack system about 10 ft left of an obvious arete up to a small roof. Pull the roof and continue up to the anchors.
F.A. Fred Henion, Chris Harmston. Summer 2002.

15. The First Time 5.9

Climb the arete above to the same anchors as Soak it Insideher. First route on the wall.
F.A. Fred Henion, Drew Hardesty. Summer 2001

Chris **Harmston on The Shield 5.11b, The Shield.** Photo: Paul Tusting

Wall of Tiers

16. Native Utard 5.10c ★★★
Climb the prow to a tricky bulge using four bolts. Move through the roof to the right, then back left and climb a crack in the face straight above the center of the roof.
F.A. Chris Harmston, Rip Griffith, Paul Tusting.

17. Diagonal Connection 5.9 ★
Start at the Trash Compactor and move right to the belay on Native Utard. All gear.
F.A. Chris Harmston, Kathy Harmston. Summer 2002

18. Trash Compactor 5.11a ★★
Start in the small cave with a large block 10 feet off the ground. Climb shattered cracks up center of the "Trash Compactor" block. Avoid the dihedral to the left and Diagonal Connection. Pull through the multiple roofs to a set of anchors. One bolt above upper roof.
F.A. Fred Henion, Rip Griffith. Summer 2002

19. Lowe Route 5.9
Climb the right-facing corner to the left of the Trash Compactor. Then traverse left onto the headwall of The Shield and to the anchors on The Sword.
F.A. Rip Griffith. Summer 2002.

20. The Sword 5.11b ★★
Climb up the shallow right facing corner past one bolt on the right side of The Shield proper. Climb the headwall above using gear to the anchors.
F.A. Chris Harmston, Rip Griffith, Paul Tusting. 8/4/02

21. The Shield 5.11b ★★★
Climb up shallow water groove past three bolts. Climb the headwall above using gear.
F.A. Chris Harmston, Paul Tusting. 8/4/02

22. Shield Evasion 5.8 ★
This route starts on a flake on the far left-side of the shield formation, then moves diagonally to the right crossing above The Shield and finishing on the anchors of The Sword.
F.A. Rip Griffith. Summer 2002

23. Greg's 5.8
Climbs the chimney/arete to the left of the route above to the anchors of The Shield.
F.A. Greg Holbrook. Summer 2002

The Attic

Wall of Tiers

The Attic
The Attic is a small cliff band (40ft) just above The Shield area. Approach it via the right edge of the talus field. This easily puts you in the ledge system at the cliff's base. Beware, if there are climbers below, there is potential for rock fall as you are moving around on the ledge. Routes described right to left.

1. Sketch Ball 5.9 R
This route climbs a shallow dihedral about 60ft right of the Test of Time arete up to a roof. There is one bolt a couple body lengths off the ground then shaky gear to the anchors below the roof.
F.A. Paul Tusting, Mike Haag. 8/11/02

2. Mike's Route 5.9
Climb Chimney about 20 ft right of the Test of Time arete with a hand crack in the back. Gear to a set of anchors.
F.A. Mike Haag, Paul Tusting. 8/11/02

3. Test of Time 5.12 (TR)
Has top-rope anchors but the lead bolts have not been installed yet.
F.A. Project

No Man's Land (No Topo or Photo)

About halfway between The Shield and The Far Side is a series of steep roofs on a second tier of rock. There are several routes in this area but information is limited.

1. Un-named 5.10d R/X ★★

This route climbs up the left-side of the first tier. It is unknown if there are anchors at the belay.
F.A. Fred Henion. Summer 2002.

2. Un-named 5.10 ★★

Climbing the route described above gains you access to a ledge system at the base of some tiered roofs. This route climbs the center of these roofs to a set of anchors.
F.A. Fred Henion. Summer 2002.

The Orange Room (No Topo or Photo)

The Orange Room is the obvious steep cleft several hundred yards to the right of the Far Side. A dangerous 5.6 scramble allows access to the routes there. These routes are quite long, steep, and sustained. Routes described right to left.

1. Orange Roughy 5.11a ★★

This route climbs the arete on the right-side of The Orange Room. There are two bolts on this route and a rack is required. Anchors are located near the lip of the steepest section of the cave. Watch the end of your rope.
F.A. Fred Henion. Summer 2003.

2. Orange Crush 5.12a ★★★

This route climbs the face to the left of Orange Roughy past two bolts then follows the hand-crack angling right past two more bolts. Anchor station is over the top. Watch the end of your rope.
F.A. Fred Henion. Summer 2003.

Uinta Rock

The Far Side

To get to this crag stay on the valley floor then head up the talus towards the corner of the cirque. From The Shield traverse at the top of the talus field. Great technical edge-climbing plus a couple of moderate cracks. Routes described right to left. A single 60m rope will get you off all of these routes.

1. Under and Over 5.11a ★★

This route is located on right-side of the main wall. The crux is at the first bolt then eases off to 5.10 although the bolts get more widely spaced. Bring a set of micronuts to protect between the bolts. Solid 5.10 climbing to anchors. 5 bolts plus anchors.
F.A. Paul Tusting, Damon, Rip Griffith. 8/17/02

2. Alien's Face 5.11c ★★

Starts just left of the obvious arch. Angle up and right past 7 bolts to anchors.
F.A. Chris Harmston, Rip Griffith. 8/11/02

3. Gary's Cows 5.11c ★★

Same start as Alien's Face but head straight up following a line of 7 bolts to the anchors on Cat Fud.
F.A. Chris Harmston, Rip Griffith. 8/11/02

4. Cat Fud 5.11b ★★

This is a line which starts right of an obvious hand crack and follows 5 bolts then gear to a set of anchors.
F.A. Chris Harmston, Rip Griffith. August 2002.

5. The Far Side 5.10 ★★★

Same anchors as route below but follows a steep finger/hand crack.
F.A. Chris Harmston, Rip Griffith. Summer 2003.

Wall of Tiers

The Far Side

6. Cat Games 5.10a ★
Start is large left-facing flake/corner system. Follow this to a roof.
Climb through it via a hand crack and clip the anchors. A 5.7 variation
goes right and then hard left to skip the roof.
F.A. Rip Griffith, Chris Harmston. 8/4/02.

7. 5.10a Arete (TR)
Very contrived: hard to keep from migrating to the crack below.
FTA. Paul Tusting. 8/17/02.

8. Decisions, Decisions 5.8+ ★
Climb a left-facing corner. A 5.10a finish is possible to the right of the
"exit" gully.
F.A. Rip Griffith, Damon. 8/17/02

9. Got My Goat 5.11b ★★

Climb towards an obvious roof with right-facing corner, follows the obvious right leaning seam. Lots of small gear and a bolt will get you to the roof. Climb through it using the corner and up to a set of anchors.

F.A. Chris Harmston, Kathy Harmston. Summer 2003.

10. Thunderbolt and Lightfoot 5.10 ★★★

Climb the clean steep face left of Got My Goat past 4 bolts and a finger crack to a set of anchors.

F.A. Chris Harmston, Eric Townsend. July 2003.

11. Unexpected Turn 5.9 ★

Find the cleft splitting a small roof about 15 feet right of Guardian Angel. Climb bulge and follow the angling crack to the right. This takes you to a right facing corner with one weird move and then up to a set of anchors.

F.A. Paul Tusting, George Jamison, Rip Griffith. 6/28/03.

Wall of Tiers

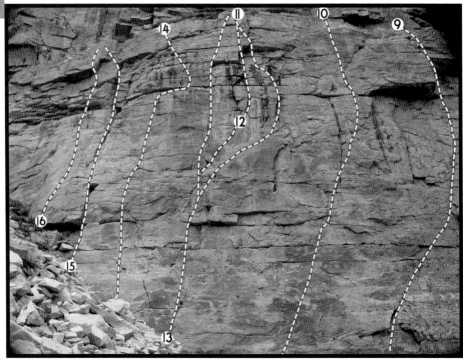

Photo: Paul Tusting

12. Sandwich 5.9

This was added after the routes above and below were climbed. It follows the same start as Unexpected Turn but follows the other crack angling to the left and heads straight up instead of moving into the corner. Shares anchors with the other routes.
F.A. Chris Harmston, Kathy Harmston. Summer 2003.

13. The Devil's Cabana Boy 5.10 ★★

Same start as Unexpected Turn, but after the initial bulge, head straight up the steep finger/hand crack to the same anchors as Unexpected Turn.
F.A. George Jamison, Rip Griffith. 6/28/03.

14. Guardian Angel 5.10a ★★

Climb the clean face 15 right of an obvious crack past three bolts to a small roof. Move right and pull the roof. Follow a seam/crack up the slab to a set of anchors. Gear is thin and tricky above the roof and on the slab, but the climbing is relatively easy. Dedicated to the memory of Sean Spinney.
F.A. Paul Tusting, Chris Harmston. July 2003.

15. Not Bad OW 5.8

Not bad for an Off-Width. Use hand jams and a #4 Camalot to overcome the chockstone. Gear to a set of anchors.
F.A. Rip Griffith, Paul Tusting. 6/28/03.

16. Hydraphobia 5.9+ ★

Climb the face to the left of the crack described above using two bolts and gear to reach a small roof. Pull over it, clip one more bolt, and then the anchors. This route shares anchors with the 5.8 crack above.
F.A. Eric Townsend, Paul Tusting. July 2003.

17. Lost Wages 5.11d ★★

Lost Wages is located on the tier directly above the Far Side. It can be accessed either by scrambling up around either side of the cliff or by topping out one of the routes. It climbs the steep north facing wall above the right- side of the Far Side. There are two bolts low on the route then gear to a set of anchors.
F.A. Fred Henion. Summer 2003.

Wall of Tiers

Wall of Tiers

Paul Tusting on The Thin Thing   5.11a, The Shield.
Photo: Chris Harmston

KEVIN C. ROGERS 2004

Photo on following Pages:
James Loveridge on Fat Ass, Pretty Face 5.10a, The Chopping Block.

Moosehorn

Moosehorn

Moosehorn

Directions: Park across the road from the Mirror Lake entrance, 25 miles from the toll booth or after mile marker 31. There is enough room on the shoulder for 4 cars. Start hiking up the abandoned section of paved road. Follow the cairns up and leftward for 10 min. You will then enter a small meadow that marks the edge of the tallus field leading to the cliffs. Depending on the wall you are heading to, expect a 15 to 20 minute approach.
USGS Map: Mirror Lake

Description: The Moosehorn area is characterized by vertical face routes with predominately small edges and is also home to some of the shortest and longest sport climbs in the Uintas. As these routes lie at the base of a large cliff, there is much potential for rockfall or even avalanches in the early season.
Elevation: 10,600 ft.

IN MEMORY OF

PAUL MOORE

"WHO LOVED
THESE MOUNTAINS"

8-7-58 TO 9-5-98

The Lowe Wall

Directions: From the meadow, follow the cairns up to the right side of the Moosehorn area. These three climbs are located on the South facing side of this outcrop.

Description: A small wall offering a few good climbs. Be sure to bring TCU's.

From Left to Right:
1. The Arete 5.10c ★
Follow cracks. Build an anchor.
F.A. Brian Cabe

2. The Face 5.11a/b ★
Up the center of the face using horizontal cracks. Build an anchor.
F.A. Brian Cabe

3. The Lowe Route 5.10d
Just left of the arete. A pair of old bolts serve as an anchor.
F.A. Rumored to be Alex Lowe

Lowe Wall

Uinto Rock

The Pico Wall

Description: This small block is located up and left of the Low Wall, and just below the Wall of Mirrors. Make sure you have a small rack when attempting these climbs as three of the four routes take gear.

1. Pico de Gallo 5.8 ★★
45 feet. 4 bolts plus anchors.
F.A. Brian Cabe, John Evans

2. Rug Rat 5.7 R
40 feet. Better than the name. All gear.
F.A. Brian Cabe, John Evans

Pico Wall

3. Pico the Good Puppy 5.8 -
35 feet. 2 bolts plus anchors. Supplimental gear.
F.A. Brian Cabe, John Evans

4. Sod Poodle 5.7
All gear.
F.A. Brian Cabe, John Evans

Wall of Mirrors

Description: Set below the main wall, this is a small cube with steep crimpy routes on the south face, and slabby moderates on the east face.

From left to right:

1. Grit 5.12b X
Solo the Arete. Pre-placing gear makes this route possible, although still thin. F.A. Dave Bell, Doug Heinrich. Summer 1998.

Wall of Mirrors

2. 5.12c/d
25 Feet. One move wonder with the crux between bolts 2 and 3. 3 bolts plus anchors.
F.A. Doug Heinrich, Drew Bedford. Summer 1998.

3. 5.12b/c
Traverse left after the 2nd bolt on Wall of Mirrors.
F.A. Doug Heinrich. Summer 1998.

4. Wall of Mirrors 5.11b ★★
32 feet. Climb the arete, then head left after the 4th bolt. 5 bolts plus anchors.
F.A. Shane Willet, Paul Moore, Mark Nakada, Doug Heinrich, Drew Bedford. Summer 1998.

Uinto Rock

Wall of Mirrors - right

Moosehorn

5. Dead Bolt 5.10c
25 feet. 2 bolts
F.A. Doug Heinrich. Summer 1998.

6. Psycho City Kid 5.10a
25 feet. 4 bolts plus anchors.
F.A. Brandon Willet, Shane Willet. Summer 1998.

7. VooDoo Billy Man 5.10a
25 feet. 4 bolts plus anchors.
F.A. Brandon Willet, Shane Willet. Summer 1998.

Moore Wall

The Moore Wall

Directions: From the edge of the meadow, go left until you see a trail heading up the talus just below Tequila.

Description: Long and techy, these climbs require good footwork.

1. Paul's Route 5.9 ★★
90 feet. A good warm-up. 13 draws.
F.A. Paul Moore, Shane Willet, Mark Nakada. Summer 1998.

2. Ray of Light 5.11c ★
90 feet. Thin and crimpy. 13 draws.
F.A. Shane Willet, Mark Nakada. Summer 1998.

3. Of Mice and Men 5.10a
90 feet. Don't go right into the chossy vegetated area. Gear to bolted anchor.
F.A. Rip Griffith. Summer 1998.

4. Mad Man of the Uinta's 5.11b ★
90 feet. Good footwork is a must. 13 Draws.
F.A. Shane Willet, Paul Moore, Mark Nakada. Summer 1998.

5. The Passage 5.7
90 feet. Start in the corner and go straight up. Expect terrible rock in the upper section. Webbing was found at mid-height in 1998.
F.A. Unknown.

6. Free Passage 5.10a ★
90 feet. Climb The Passage and branch right just above the prominent ledge at the top.
F.A. Rip Griffith, Drew Hardesty. Summer 1998.

7. Don't Tell Jonny 5.10c ★★
100 feet. Start just a few feet right of the corner crack. 14 draws.
F.A. Shane Willet, Paul Moore, Mark Nakada. Summer 1998.

8. Wish You Were Here 5.10b ★★
90 feet. A great climb with a surprising amount of exposure. Head onto the arete when in doubt. 12 draws.
F.A. Shane Willet, Paul Moore, Mark Nakada. Summer 1998.

9. Project 5.12b/c
Direct start to Tequila. Gear and one bolt to the roof. Has only been toproped.
F.A.

10. Tequila 5.12b ★★
100 feet. Place tcu's and stoppers at the start, then bolts after the roof.
F.A. Drew Bedford, Doug Heinrich. Summer 1998.

11. Project
100 feet.
F.A.

Lower Moore Wall
Directions: Right of Tequilla and above the Wall of Mirrors.

Moosehorn

Lower Moore Wall

1. Bullwinkle 5.10c ★★
90 ft. Climb a thin crack in a right-facing corner system about 100 ft left of Root Down. Push out a mantle when the crack ends. Gear to a set of chains.
F.A. Chris Harmston, Paul Tusting. 7/21/02

2. Natasha 5.10a ★
90 ft. Climb the face about 20 ft left of the dihedral described below. Place gear in the horizontals and climb up to the anchors, which are shared with the route above.
F.A. Chris Harmston, Paul Tusting. 7/21/02

3. Root Down 5.9+ ★★
50 ft. This route climbs a hand crack that passes through two roofs on a small south facing pillar above the Wall of Mirrors. Standard rack easily protects this pitch to a set of anchors.
F.A. Paul Tusting, Chris Harmston. 7/21/02

4. Not Worthy 5.10
Top rope the arete to the right of Root Down from the same anchors. Not worthy of bolts but a way to get some extra mileage for the day.
FTA. Paul Tusting, Chris Harmston. 7/21/02

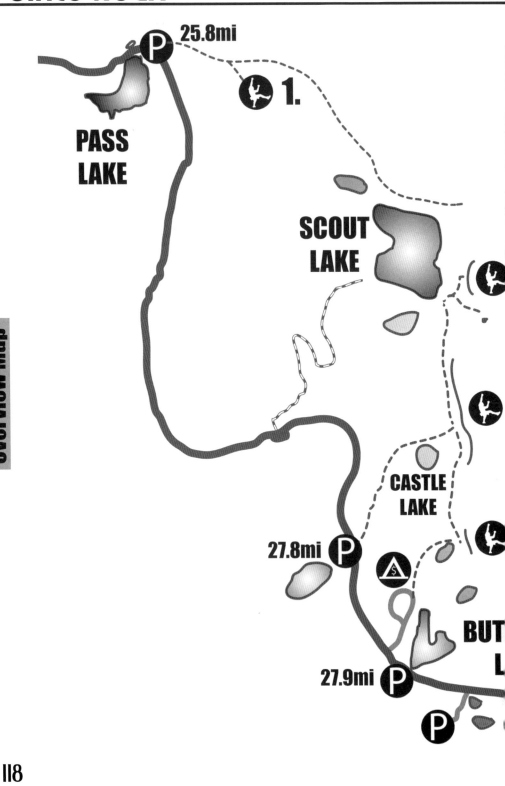

PASS LAKE

25.8mi

1.

SCOUT LAKE

CASTLE LAKE

27.8mi

27.9mi

BUT
L

OVERVIEW MAP 5

**N
O
R
T
H**

1. PICTURESQUE WALL
2. SCOUT LAKE
3. CASTLE LAKE
4. BUTTERFLY LAKE
5. RUTH LAKE

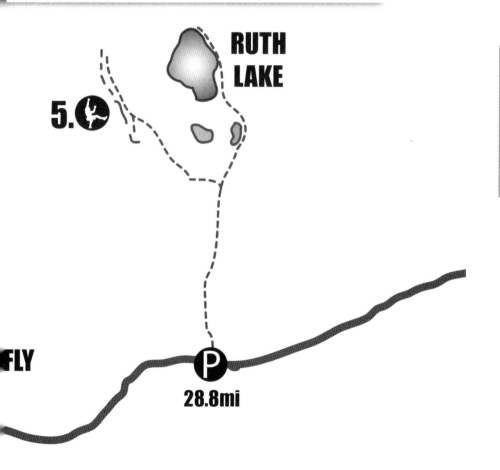

RUTH
LAKE

5.

FLY

P
28.8mi

Uinto Rock

Picturesque Wall

Description: While only a few "established" climbs exist, there are many toprope variations. The top of the cliff is easily accessible to set up anchors. This "picturesque" cliff overlooks Reids and Baldy peaks and is a great spot to watch the sun set.

Directions: Park at the Pass Lake/ Lofty Lake Trailhead 25.8 miles from the tollbooth or just after mile marker 32. Hike towards Lofty Lake. In approximately 10 minutes, you will see a small cliff band on your right hand side. There is a discreet trail leading to the cliffs.
USGS Map: Mirror Lake

From left to right.

1. Block Route 5.9
30 feet. The furthest left route on the wall. Has a loose block halfway up the wall. All gear to a bolted anchor.
FFA. Ray Dahl. Summer 1991

2. Shorty 5.10c or V1
15 feet. Toprope or just boulder.
FA. Unknown

3. A Dream Within a Dream 5.10a
40 feet. Three bolts of good climbing.
FFA. Ray Dahl. Summer 1991

Picturesque Wall

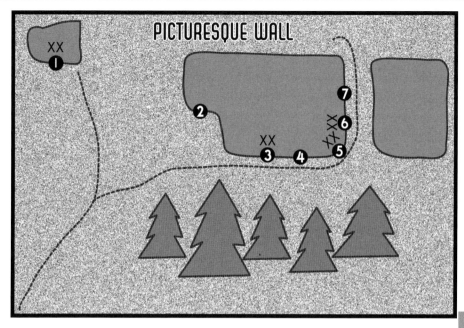

4. Turbo Force 5.10d
40 feet. Thin and crimpy.
FTA. Ray Dahl, Kip Henrey. Summer 1991

5. E Tu Brute 5.8
35 feet. Climb the arête.
FTA. Ray Dahl. Summer 1991

6. Raven 5.9 R
35 feet.
FFA. Ray Dahl. Summer 1991

7. 5.9 TR
35 feet.
FFA. Ray Dahl. Summer 1991

Photo on following pages:
Paul Tusting on Modest Yuppie 5.11d, Purgatory Wall.

Scout Lake

Scout Lake

Book Cliffs

Description: Set above Scout Lake at 10,300 feet, the Book Cliffs overlook some of the most scenic views of any of the Uinta crags. With 26 climbs that are easily accessible for toproping, this is a great area for the moderate climber, but also has many harder climbs. Be prepared with a rack, as the majority of the climbs here use natural pro. The Scouts lease this land, but CANNOT restrict access. If you have any access problems at this cliff, please alert the Access Fund as well as the Kamas Ranger District. During July and August the Scouts use a small section of the cliff for their climbing program. If the climbs are being used, please do not disturb them. There are many other climbs to do to the left. Climbers have been visiting this area since at least 1968. We have tried to be as accurate as possible with first ascent information but are sure that some of the first ascents are probably first known ascents.
Elevation: 10,300 ft.

Directions: 27.8 miles from the tollbooth and just a few hundred yards past (when heading west) the Camp Steiner road turnoff is a paved road heading off to the right with boulders blocking it from extending very far. Park here, cross the street, and head north up a subtle drainage. Soon you will get to Castle Lake. Once at the lake, walk around to the north side (closest to the cliffs) and then follow the trail west past the Steiner Rifle Range and then to the foot of Scout Lake. Here you will find the Scout's campfire bowl. Walk up the center of this and follow the trail to the cliffs. Approach should take 30-45 minutes. Please remember that you are passing through land

leased by the Boy Scouts and access could be lost through someone's careless behavior.
USGS Map: Mirror Lake

From left to right.

1. Pale Rider 5.10 ★ (not on topo)
50 feet. Handcrack through small roof to natural anchor. Gear to #1 Camalot
F.A. Nathan Smith, Chad Jolley. 8/3/00

2. Harsh Reality 5.12a ★
50 feet. Finger crack out an 8 foot roof. Boulder problem on gear. Turns to 5.6 after the roof. Sling the pine for the anchor. Gear to #3 (orange) Metolius.
F.A. Nathan Smith. July 2000

3. Clear and Present Danger 5.10c PG ★★
60 feet. Follow the shallow seam up the face past one bolt, to a large horizontal break. Trend leftwards through the seam after the horizontal. First done without the bolt. Gear up to #2 Camalot, but mostly small gear. Bolted anchors.
FTA James Taylor, Carl Begal. Summer 1993   FFA. Nathan Smith. Summer 1998.

Brandon Fallahi on Novicane
5.9, Scout Lake

4. A Fungus Among Us 5.10c PG

60 feet. Climb past 2 well-spaced bolts to the offwidth filled with lichen and moss. Better as a toprope. Gear to #5 Camalot. Bolted anchor.

FTA. James Taylor, Carl Begal. Summer 1993. FFA. Nathan Smith 2000.

5. Shinangwav 5.11b/c ★★

Means Coyote in Paiute. 60 feet. Climb the slightly overhung blank-looking face. Techy. 4 bolts and gear to #3 (orange) Metolius. Bolted anchor.

FA. Nathan Smith. 9/20/01

6. Hucks Fin 5.10b ★★

60 feet. Follow up the open book arete. Gear to black Metolius. Natural Anchor.

FA. Unknown

7. Guillotine 5.10b ★★

70 feet. Scramble through 20 feet of 4th class, to a beautiful, slightly overhanging face. 5 bolts and bolted anchor. Yellow Metolius protects the initial moves to the first bolt.

FA. John Rogers. Summer 1998.

8. Blues Streak 5.10b ★★

80 feet. Scramble through 20 feet of 4th class, to a beautiful slightly overhanging face. Start on Guillotine and cut right after the first bolt to the blue water streak. 5 bolts and anchors. Yellow Metolius protects the initial moves to the first bolt.

FA. Nathan Smith. 9/15/01.

9. Green Eggs and Ham 5.8 PG ★★★

70 feet. Climb the green face through perfect rock. Can be tricky to protect. All small size (up to .75") cams to a bolted anchor.

FA. James Taylor. Summer 1993.

10. A-Climb-A-Tize 5.8 ★

60 feet. Follow the arete 8 feet left of Novocain. All gear. Natural anchor.

FA. John Rogers and Ryan Neilson. Summer 1998.

11. Novocain 5.8 ★★★

60 feet. Follow the vertical crack through a small roof to more face climbing. Gear to #3 Camalot. Hexes protect this climb best. Natural anchor.
FA. James Taylor, Carl Begal. Summer 1993.

12. Ed's Route 5.8 PG ★

Start in the shallow open book just 6 feet right of Novocain. Trend up and leftwards, joining Novocain towards the top. Hard to protect. All small gear (up to .75") until joining Novocain.
FA. Ed Fallis, Nathan Smith. September 2001.

13. Lustography 5.10b R ★★ (Not on Topo)
30 feet. Just 10 feet right of #12. Steeper than it looks. A fall clipping the 2nd bolt would be bad. The slab to the left is off route. 2 bolts to bolted anchor. Drilled by hand.
FA. Nathan Smith. Summer 1998.

Climbs 14-18 are used by the Scouts during the summer. If they are being used, please do not try to climb them. There are many other routes to do.

14. A Separate Peace 5.7 ★
30 feet. The far left-hand side of the scout wall. May be in use on weekdays during July and August. Small gear. Bolted anchor on top.
FA. Kevin Rogers, B.J. Minson. Summer 1998.

15. 5.7 ★
30 feet. Middle route on the scout wall. All thin gear. Bolted anchor on top.
FA. Unknown.

16. Gone With the Wind 5.7 ★★
30 feet. Climb the thin face just right of the arete. All thin gear. Bolted anchor on top.
FA. Kevin Rogers, Cheri Smith, Nathan Smith. Summer 1998.

Scout Lake

ACCESS: IT'S EVERYONE'S CONCERN

The Access Fund is a national nonprofit climbers' organization working to keep climbing areas open and conserve the climbing environment. Need help with a climbing related issue? Call us and please consider these principles when climbing.

- **ASPIRE TO CLIMB WITHOUT LEAVING A TRACE:** Especially in environmentally sensitive areas like caves. Chalk can be a significant impact. Pick up litter and leave trees and plants intact.
- **MAINTAIN A LOW PROFILE:** Minimize noise and yelling at the crag.
- **DISPOSE OF HUMAN WASTE PROPERLY:** Use toilets whenever possible. If toilets are not available, dig a "cat hole" at least six inches deep and 200 feet from any water, trails, campsites or the base of climbs. Always pack out toilet paper. Use a "poop tube" on big wall routes.
- **USE EXISTING TRAILS:** Cutting switchbacks causes erosion. When walking off-trail, tread lightly, especially in the desert on cryptogamic soils.
- **BE DISCRETE WITH FIXED ANCHORS:** Bolts are controversial and are not a convenience. Avoid placing unless they are absolutely necessary. Camouflage all anchors and remove unsightly slings from rappel stations.
- **RESPECT THE RULES:** Speak up when other climbers do not. Expect restrictions in designated wilderness areas, rock art sites and caves. Power drills are illegal in wilderness and all national parks.
- **PARK AND CAMP IN DESIGNATED AREAS:** Some climbing areas require a permit for overnight camping.
- **RESPECT PRIVATE PROPERTY:** Be courteous to landowners.
- **JOIN THE ACCESS FUND:** To become a member, make a tax-deductible donation of $35.

P.O. Box 17010
Boulder, CO 80308
303.545.6772

ACCESS FUND
your climbing future
www.accessfund.org

17. Hero Maker 5.11a ★★

40 feet. Use the arete up this thin face. Spectacular view. 4 bolts to bolted anchor.
FA. Nathan Smith. Summer 1999

18. Unnamed 5.6 ★

20 feet. Short face to bolted anchor on top.
FA. James Taylor, Doug Smith. Summer 1994.

19. Jabba 5.10 (Not on topo)

30 feet. This is located on the east side of the detached block in the center of the wall. Climb through a small roof. All gear.
Matt Deming, James Taylor, Dan Smith. Summer 1998.

The Purgatory Wall

Directions: Routes 20-26 are located up the hill 200 meters and to the right of the main wall.

Description: This wall is steep, juggy and is in the shade until late afternoon.
Elevation: 10,500 ft.

From left to right:

20. Pink Soldier 5.12a ★★

70 feet. Start next to Corporate Hippy and climb up and left staying right above the slab. Climb past 4 bolts to an anchor, making big moves all the way. You can either solo the 1st 20 feet, or scramble up the slab and pre-clip the 1st bolt.
FA. Nathan Smith. 6/04/02

21. Var. Pink Hippy 5.12 ★★

22. Corporate Hippy 5.11d ★★

60 feet. Follow the steep line up the center of the wall angling towards the arete at the top. Stick clip the 1st bolt, or bring some small cams to protect the start. Follow past 5 bolts to anchor. This climb was drilled by hand.
FA. Nathan Smith. 10/07/98

23. Var. Corporate Soldier 5.12 ★★

24. Modest Yuppie 5.11d ★★
60 feet. Start at the base of the arete and follow it all the way to the top, joining Corporate Hippy for the last 2 bolts. Small cams are needed to protect the horizontal crack above the 1st bolt. The purple 2Cam works well. FA. Nathan Smith. 6/4/02

25. Var. Modest Soldier 5.12 ★★

26. Hippy Climber 5.8 PG ★★
60 feet. Climb the slab staying 4-8 feet from the arete. This climb is hard to protect, and has amazing exposure. Small cams. Shares the anchor for #24. This climb is best to have someone follow and clean. The first ascentionists were able to place Splitter Gear 2Cams in spots you could not protect otherwise.
FA. Mike Haag, Nathan Smith. 6/4/02

Scout Lake

Mike Haag on Corporate Hippy 5.11d, Purgatory Wall

Castle Lake

Description: Castle Lake has a host of short and fun climbs and has a southern exposure, receiving sun most of the day. The Chopping Block is south & east facing.
Elevation: 10,400 ft.

Directions: 27.8 miles from the tollbooth and just a few hundred yards past (when heading west) the Camp Steiner road turnoff is a paved road heading off to the right with boulders blocking it from extending very far. Park here, cross the street, and head north up a subtle drainage. Soon you will get to Castle Lake, head up hill to the cliffs above. Approach should take about 20 minutes.
USGS Map: Mirror Lake

1. Prodigal Son 5.8 ★★
This climb was done as two separate pitches but can be run together as one. Follow the open book for the upper pitch.
F.A. James Taylor, Ben Anderson, Matt Deming. Summer 1995.

2. Shoeless 5.8 ★
F.A. James Taylor, Ben Anderson, Matt Deming. Summer 1995.

3. Unnamed 5.6 ★★
Follow the 2-3" crack on the slab.
F.A. Dave Smith 1968?

4. Wife and 2 Kids 5.7 ★
F.A. James Taylor, Ben Anderson, Matt Deming. Summer 1995.

Castle Lake

Tobacco Wall

This is the main wall above Castle Lake with a prominent right-facing corner. Routes described from left to right. Routes are about 60 ft in length.

5. Ibuprofen 5.11a
Climb up the shallow left-facing corner on the left edge of the cliff. Put in gear or clip pins at the roof and pull up and around to the left. Traverse right and clip the pin and second bolt. Avoids the crux of Morphine but shares the anchors.
F.A. Bryan Beavers. Summer 2001.

6. Morphine (A.K.A. Numchucks) 5.12+
Climb up the center of the face placing thin gear. Head up the roof and clip a bolt. A BIG toss will get you through this move and on to the bolt and anchors above.
F.A. Clay Calhoun. 7/10/02.

7. Tobacco 5.10d ★
Follow two cracks in a right-facing corner to a ledge. Climb through the roof using a vertical seam and clip the anchors.
F.A. Mike Springsteen, Bryan Beavers. Summer 2001.

The Following routes are located at the far right side of the Castle Lake cliff band.

8. Unnamed 5.8
Climb the short crack.
F.A. Dan Smith, James Taylor, Lincoln Seals

9. Unnamed 5.9
Climb the short crack.
F.A. James Taylor, Dan Smith, Lincoln Seals

10. London Bridges 5.8 ★
Two bolts to anchors, along with supplemental gear.
F.A. Jeff Baldwin. 2002

11. The Straw 5.10b ★
7 bolts to anchors, along with a tcu protect this line.
F.A. Jeff Baldwin. 2002

12. Crumble Cake 5.11b ★★
7 bolts to anchor. Stay on the Arete
F.A. Jeff Baldwin. 2002

13. Cemetery Gates 5.10a ★
Start right of the detached block at the start. Two bolts and a full rack of stoppers and cams up to #2 Camalot.
F.A. Jeff Baldwin. 2002

Castle Lake

14. Thor's Unhappy 5.10a ★★★

Mix one part torrential downpour, a ravenous first ascentionist covered in carabiners and drilling equipment and one of the most intense lightning storms, then take a guess where the name came from. Bolts, a small/medium cam and a great finish.
F.A. Jeff Baldwin. 2002

15. Hair Raiser 5.7 ★

Follow the prominent black streak. Mixed line.
F.A. Jeff Baldwin. 2002

Castle Lake

Jeff Baldwin on Crumble Cake 5.11b, Castle Lake
Photo: Jeff Baldwin collection

Uinta Rock

Chopping Block

To get to the Chopping Block from Castle Lake, follow the ledge system to your left. This cliff is only about 50 ft high but packs a punch and has some amazing rock. Routes described from left to right.

1. Another Way Up 5.8
Climb up the right side of the south-facing wall on gear. No anchors, walk off.
F.A. Bryan Beavers, Paul Tusting. 7/17/02

2. Fat Ass, Pretty Face 5.10 ★
Climb up through the blocks just left of the prow. You will be rewarded with great thin face climbing. Gear climbing to the anchors on the arête below.
F.A. James Loveridge, Paul Tusting. 10/13/02

3. .38 Special 5.12a ★
Start right of the arête. Follow horizontals to one bolt. Pull hard and climb to the anchors. Gear and one bolt to anchors.
F.A. Bryan Beavers, Clay Calhoun. 7/27/02

4. The Death of Democracy 5.12a R ★
Climb right up the center of the face clipping one bolt as you go. The one heinous move is well protected. Anchors are straight above. The history of the fixed bong above the anchors is unknown.
F.A. Clay Calhoun, Bryan Beavers. 7/27/02

5. Don't Take Your Guns to Town 5.10d ★★
Follow the obvious seam up through a bulge then onto a tenuous slab. Three bolts to the same anchors as the route above.
F.A. Bryan Beavers, Paul Tusting. 7/17/02.

6. Green With Envy 5.11- R
Shorter than the routes to the left. Follows a green streak up the wall to anchors. A good TR or a silly lead. Easier if you stay right.
F.A. Clay Calhoun, Summer 2002

Castle Lake

7. Laryngitis 5.4 ★

Climb the west-facing slab across from the Chopping Block. A good first gear lead. No anchors, walk off.
F.A. Nathan Smith (Solo). 10/13/02

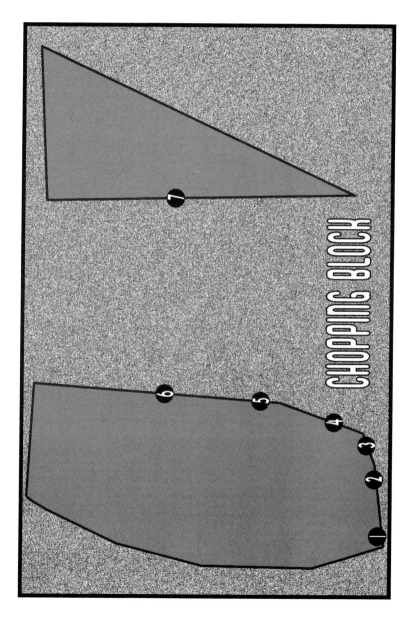

Uinto Rock

Butterfly Lake

Butterfly Lake

Description: Butterfly lake is a series of disconnected short cliffs. The routes are a good supplement to a day at Castle Lake. They are mostly south facing.
Elevation: 10,400 ft.

Directions: Park at Butterfly Lake, 27.9 miles from the toll booth or after mile marker 34. If this parking lot is full, there is a pullout on the right 27.8 miles from the tollbooth. Follow the right edge of the lake until you are across from where you parked. Go into a grove of trees and out into another meadow with a small pond. Just above, you will find a short, steep, and solid buttress. You can also traverse east from Castle Lake. Plan on 10-15 min.
USGS Map: Hayden Peak and Mirror Lake

Routes described left to right.

1. Brief Case 5.11c ★
Short but sweet. Climb through two roofs on thin gear about 100 ft left of the Butterfly Lake Crag.
F.A. Bryan Beavers, Paul Tusting. 7/10/02

2. Dirty Secrets 5.7
Climb up a crack, then move right to the arete. Finish up through a corner. Same anchors as Humble Pie.
F.A. Paul Tusting, Cathy Beavers, Alexia. 7/13/02

Butterfly Lake

3. Humble Pie 5.9+ ★
Just around the corner from Double Roof. Climb the steep east-facing wall to anchors. F.A. Paul Tusting, Clay Calhoun (Solo), Bryan Beavers (Solo). 7/13/02

These three routes are about 100 ft right of the cliff described above.

4. Flesh Wound 5.10a R/X
Climb shallow crack just left of the route above. Clip the same anchors as #5. F.A. Clay Calhoun, Bryan Beavers. 7/13/02

5. Short Lived 5.10d ★
Just left of the route above. Climb up and clip one bolt then follow the crack to the top.
F.A. Bryan Beavers, Paul Tusting, Clay Calhoun. 7/10/02.

6. Baby Thor 5.10d/11a ★
Climb up a right-facing corner until a bolt on the arete to your left can be clipped. Move under it and up to the anchors.
F.A. Bryan Beavers, Paul Tusting, Clay Calhoun. 7/10/02.

Butterfly Lake

Heath Christensen on Black Elk 5.10a, Ruth Lake

Ruth Lake

Ruth Lake

Description: With 6 separate walls, and 56 routes, Ruth Lake offers climbing for almost any ability level. Vertical faces abound with small roofs thrown in here and there. The holds tend to be very positive and skin friendly. On weekends, the Good Medicine Wall tends to fill up quickly, but the other walls usually offer uncrowded climbing. With the exception of the Chief wall, and the last three climbs on the Good Medicine Wall, the Ruth Lake routes are in the shade for most of the day making them a great mid-summer choice.
Elevation: 10,500 ft.

Directions: There are 2 paved parking areas on the west side of the road located just before and at mile marker 35. 28.8 miles from the tollbooth. There is a toilet at the upper parking lot. Overflow parking is located on the east side of the road. The trail starts at the lower parking area next to the information kiosk. Hike East for about 1/2 mile. 100 yards after you pass the "Haymakers and Hibernators" interpretive sign and 20 feet before you come to the "Adaptation: Key to survival" interpretive sign, take the smaller trail to the left. Follow this trail through a grove of pines and over a glacial polished rock formation to the base of The Good Medicine Wall.
USGS Map: Mirror Lake and Hayden Peak

**Dr. Harry Adelson
Don Yah-Keerah
5.7, Ruth Lake**

The Chief Wall

Description: The newest addition to Ruth Lake, the Chief Wall offers secluded moderate climbing. The walls are vertical to slightly less than vertical in nature.

Directions: Follow the trail to The Good Medicine Wall. Once there head east along the base of the cliff and through a talus field to the wall.

1. Yah-Keerah (Chief Walker) 5.7 ★★
40 feet. A great finger crack that will rarely be climbed because it requires gear. Take a rack of stoppers and gear up to 1". One bolt at the start plus anchors.
F.A. Nathan Smith, Harry Adelson. 9/14/02

2. Tatanka-Iyotanka (Sitting Bull) 5.10b ★★
45 feet. Start under a small roof and pull onto the face above. 5 bolts plus anchors.
F.A. Nathan Smith. 9/02/02

Ruth Lake

3. Hin-mah-too-yah-lat-kekt (Chief Joseph) 5.10d ★
45 feet. Start in the black streak. The second bolt is not in an ideal position due to poor rock below it. Hang the 2nd draw with a stick clip. 5 bolts plus anchors.
F.A. Nathan Smith. 9/02/02

4. General George Custer 5.10
40 feet. A judgment error by the first ascensionist. This route has everything, but you don't want any of it. Unless you want to tick the wall, skip this one. 4 bolts plus anchors.
F.A. Nathan Smith. 9/14/02

5. Makhpiya-Luta (Red Cloud) 5.10b ★
40 feet. Start in the pockets and head up and left. Harder than it looks. 3 bolts plus anchors.
F.A. Nathan Smith. 9/14/02

Photo on following pages:
Britton Woolf on Hero Maker 5.11a, Scout Lake

Good Medicine Wall

Description: The Good Medicine Wall holds some of the best climbs in the area. It is also one of the most crowded walls in the Uintas because of this. The routes vary from short 6 bolt climbs, to long 13 bolt endurance leads.

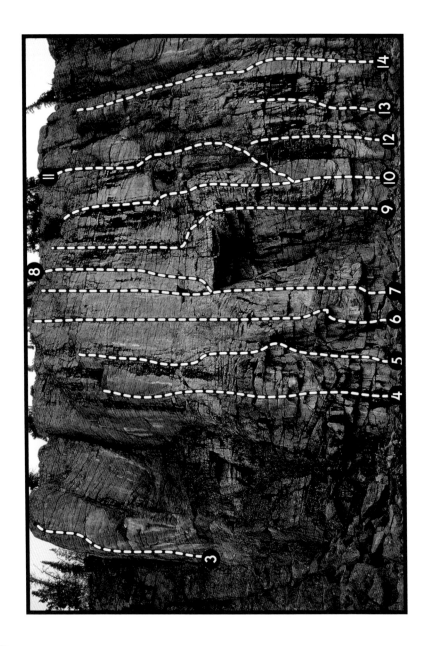

Ruth Lake

This climb is located 50 yards left of climbs 2 and 3.

1. Adore 5.11a ★ (Not on topo)

40 feet. Mixed climb. 3 bolts plus gear up to 1". One bolt for the anchor. Walk off.

F.A. Jeff Baldwin. Summer 2001

2. Spirit Guide 5.12a (Not on topo)

50 feet. Shares 1st bolt with Good Medicine. Follow the tan hangers on the left side of the arete. 9 bolts plus anchors.

F.A. Jim Stone.

3. Good Medicine 5.12a ★★

50 feet. Start in the corner and head up the funky crack. Just after the top of the crack, punch straight up the arete. 7 bolts plus anchors.

F.A. Jim Stone. Summer 1996

4. Vision Quest 5.11b

55 feet. An awkward and steep start leads to "mountaineering" climbing before the final 3 bolts of face climbing. 9 bolts plus anchors.

F.A. Jim Stone. Summer 1996

5. Sacred Hoop 5.10a ★

62 feet. Awkward stemming leads to a good headwall and finger locks above. 9 bolts plus anchors.

F.A. Jim Stone. Summer 1996

6. Dream Catcher 5.11c ★★

70 feet. The technical crux is right off the ground. Use a good spotter to get to the first bolt, or stick clip. The climbing is much easier until the headwall where the redpoint crux is still lurking. 13 bolts plus anchors.

F.A. Jim Stone. Summer 1996

7. Wind Walker 5.11c ★★

70 feet. Jug climbing to an amazing crimpy headwall. 12 bolts plus anchors.

F.A. Jim Stone. Summer 1996

Ruth Lake

8. Moon Stone 5.11b ★★

70 feet. Same start as Wind Walker, but bust right halfway up. 12 bolts plus anchors.
F.A. Jim Stone. Summer 1996

9. Black Elk 5.10a ★★★

75 feet. One of the best climbs on the wall. Climb past 9 bolts through perfect rock, to bolted anchors.
F.A. Jeff Baldwin. Summer 2001

10. White Mans Burden 5.10b/c R

70 feet. Start in the fist sized crack and climb through varying terrain. A bit sporty to the anchors. Bring a full rack. Gear with bolted anchors.
F.A. Rip Griffith. Summer 1997

11. Chocolate Moose 5.10a ★

70 feet. Use the same start as White Mans Burden, then angle right to the anchors of Bear Dance. Pass the anchors and keep climbing straight above. Bring a full rack. Gear and bolted anchors.
Jeff Baldwin. Summer 2001

12. The Bear Dance 5.10c ★

40 feet. If you can get off the ground, fight the pump through easier climbing above. 5 bolts plus anchors.
F.A. Jim Stone. Summer 1996

13. Ghost Dance 5.12b ★★★

40 feet. A thin and crimpy start leads to slightly easier climbing in the black streak midway. 6 bolts plus anchors.
F.A. Jim Stone. Summer 1996

14. Tomahawk in the Back 5.10b ★

70 feet. Start in a chossy looking crack then stay just to the left of the crack. You will find a couple of nice no-hands rests before the final roof. 8 bolts plus anchors.
F.A. Jim Stone.

Ruth Lake

Addy Sage on Guillotine 5.10b, Scout Lake

15. Indian Summer 5.10a/b

63 feet. Start in the chimney and finish on the left arete. 8 bolts plus anchors.

F.A. Shane Willet, Paul Moore, Mark Nakada. Summer 1996

16. Medicine Man 5.10d

63 feet. Climb the double finger cracks to a no-hands rest before scrambling up to the right-hand arete above. 8 bolts plus anchors.

F.A. Jim Stone. Summer 1996

17. I am Haunted 5.10d ★

45 feet. Steeper than it looks. Be careful of the glued chosspile about 3/4 of the way up. 8 bolts plus anchors.

F.A. Shane Willet, Paul Moore, Mark Nakada. Summer 1996

18. Tribal Warfare 5.10b ★

55 feet. Start off in a stemming corner then pull onto the face above. The glued undercling in the crux could come off at any time. 8 bolts plus anchors.

F.A. Shane Willet, Paul Moore, Mark Nakada. Summer 1996

19. Wounded Knee 5.10c ★★

65 feet. A great climb with no real crux. Watch out for the pump. 7 bolts plus anchors.

F.A. Shane Willet, Paul Moore, Mark Nakada. Summer 1996

20. The Legend 5.10c ★★★

50 feet. One of the best on the wall. Pull through a series of roofs with great rests in between. 7 bolts plus anchors.

F.A. Shane Willet, Paul Moore, Mark Nakada. Summer 1996

21. Forgotten Warrior 5.11c ★

55 feet. A climb with two distinct cruxes separated by great rests. The first crux is tendon blowing thin and the second is a powerful roof. 7 bolts plus anchors.

F.A. Scott Tiber. Summer 1996

Ruth Lake

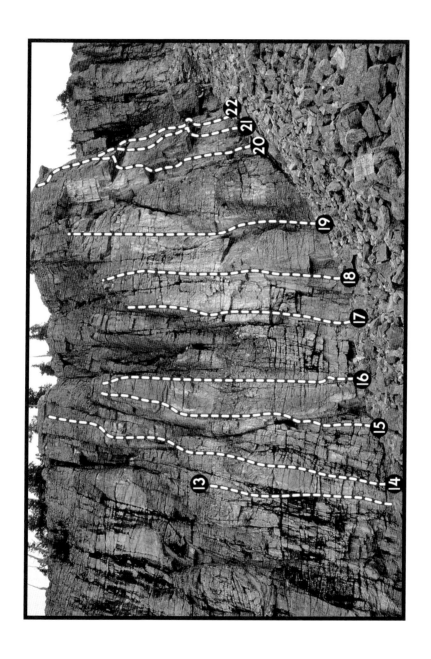

22. Peace Treaty 5.9 ★★★
50 feet. Great climbing with the crux pulling the roof 3/4 of the way up. 6 bolts plus anchors.
F.A. Shane Willet, Paul Moore, Mark Nakada. Summer 1996

23. Fire Water 5.7 ★★
30 feet. Start on a good ledge and climb past great edges. 4 bolts plus anchors.
F.A. Shane Willet, Mark Nakada. Summer 1996

24. Sun Dog 5.8 ★★
30 feet. 4 bolts plus anchors.
F.A. Shane Willet, Mark Nakada. Summer 1996

Black Diamond™

801.278.5533 · www.BlackDiamondEquipment.com

Last Stand Wall

Description: This small wall offers a good range of climbing for the day. Your warm-up, projects and warm-downs can all be found right here.

Directions: 50 meters Right of Sun Dog is the Last Stand Wall.

Ruth Lake

Last Stand Wall

1. Crescent Moon 5.8 ★★

50 feet. The left-most route on the wall, Crescent Moon climbs a clean slab with tan bolt hangers that are hard to see. 8 bolts plus anchors. F.A. Shane Willet, Mark Nakada. Summer 1996

2. Peyote Trip 5.9 ★

60 feet. Start just right of the arete, and change aspects a third of the way up. 9 bolts plus anchors. F.A. Shane Willet, Mark Nakada. Summer 1996

3. The Last Stand 5.11a ★★

60 feet. Climb past two bolts, then head left up the arete at the small roofs. Shares anchors with Peyote Trip. 8 bolts plus anchors. F.A. Jim Stone. Summer 1996

4. Fist Full of Scalps 5.11c ★★
50 feet. The same start as Last Stand, but keep going straight up. 8 bolts plus anchors.
F.A. Jim Stone. Summer 1996

5. Scalp Fest 5.10d ★★
60 feet. Climb through bulges and small roofs to a narrow face. 9 bolts plus anchors.
F.A. Shane Willet, Paul Moore, Mark Nakada. Summer 1996

6. Sweat Lodge 5.10b ★
50 feet. Climb through chossy looking rock to a roof. Pull the roof on the right. 9 bolts plus anchors.
F.A. Shane Willet, Paul Moore, Mark Nakada. Summer 1996

Warrior Wall

Directions: Head 50 yards up and right of the Last Stand wall to reach the Warrior Wall.

Description: The climbs on this wall tend to be thin, crimpy and slightly over vertical.

1. Pale Face Blunder 5.9 (Not on topo)
40 feet. This climb starts just left of Pale Face Plunder. Mossy crack and face to a natural anchor. All gear.
F.A. C.J. Whittaker, Greg Davis. Summer 2003

2. Pale Face Plunder 5.9 (Not on topo)
40 feet. This climb starts 20 feet left of Silent Warrior. Start in the shallow chimney. Bring a full rack 1/4" to 3". Gear plus bolted anchors.
F.A. Rip Griffith, Kevin Fosberg, Shane Willet. Summer 1996.

3. Silent Warrior 5.10a/b R

35 feet. Start five feet right of a crack. A bit sporty without supplemental gear. 3 bolts plus anchors.
F.A. Jim Stone. Summer 1997

4. Cry of the Warrior 5.11c R

35 feet. Shares the anchor with Silent Warrior. Climbing from the 3rd to fourth bolt is runout without supplemental gear. 4 bolts plus anchors.
F.A. Jim Stone. Summer 1997

Ruth Lake

Warrior Wall

5. Rain Dance 5.10d ★

30 feet. Edgy. 5 bolts plus anchors.
F.A. Shane Willet, Mark Nakada. Summer 1996

6. Four Knuckled Warrior 5.10c ★

40 feet. Start just left of the corner. No-hands rest 3/4 of the way up. 6 bolts plus anchors.
F.A. Shane Willet, Mark Nakada. Summer 1996

7. Dog Man 5.11d ★★★
50 feet. A thin start leads to a rest 15 feet up. Climb the arete above and then onto the left face. 7 bolts plus anchors.
F.A. Jim Stone. Summer 1997

8. Warrior Without a Cause 5.12b ★★
50 feet. A bouldery crux between bolts 2 and 3 lead to easier climbing above, but beware of pumping out at the powerful roof. 7 bolts plus anchors.
F.A. Jim Stone. Summer 1997

9. Blood of the Warrior 5.10d ★
60 feet. Stick clip the first bolt. A thin start leads to easier climbing in the middle. A good rest is found just before the anchors. 6 bolts plus anchors.
F.A. Jim Stone. Summer 1997

10. This Game of Ghosts 5.11a ★
60 feet. A harder start to Blood of the Warrior. 7 bolts plus anchors.
F.A. Shane Willet, Paul Moore. Summer 1997

11. Broken Treaty 5.10b
60 feet. Follow the left-angling crack for 40 feet, then angle right to The Last Warrior's anchors. Bring a full rack. Gear plus anchors.
F.A. Kevin Fosberg. Summer 1997

12. The Last Warrior 5.10b ★
60 feet. Follow the large black streak to a rest before the anchors. 7 bolts plus anchors.
F.A. Shane Willet, Mark Nakada. Summer 1997

Ruth Lake

Jeff Baldwin on the first ascent of Black Elk 5.10a, Ruth Lake

Assassin Wall

Directions: Just down and right of the Warrior Wall.
Description: This wall is mainly less then vertical with a few small bulges.

Assassin Wall

1. Power Boy 5.8 ★
57 feet. Climb the funky ramp onto the face above. A mantle 3/4 of the way up could give some trouble. 8 bolts plus anchors.
F.A. Shane Willet, Paul Moore. Summer 1997

2. Uinta Hit Squad 5.9 ★
70 feet. Steep jugs turn into crimpy face climbing on the headwall above. 9 bolts plus anchors.
F.A. Shane Willet, Paul Moore. Summer 1996

Ruth Lake

3. Don't Question Me or I'll Kill You Right Now! 5.10a ★
70 feet. A steep start leads to techy face climbing above. 8 bolts plus anchors.
F.A. Shane Willet, Paul Moore. Summer 1996

4. Bring on the Clowns 5.6 ★
60 feet. A good first lead. 6 bolts plus anchors.
F.A. Brandon Willet

Uinta Rock

Memorial Wall

Directions: 50-100 feet right of Bring on the Clowns.
Description: A good mix of sport and trad routes. Bring a rack.

1. Skyler's Arete 5.11b ★
40 feet. Hug the arete for 4 bolts, before getting a no-hands at the base of the roof. Punch the roof and make the easy run-out to the anchors. 5 bolts plus anchors.
F.A. Skyler. Summer 2002

2. Chop This! 5.10a
40 feet. Gear 3/8" to 2.5". Ends on the ledge halfway.
F.A. Rip Griffith, Cathy Pollock.

3. Chopping Block 5.10a
40 feet. Gear to #4 Camalot. No anchors.
F.A. Rip Griffith.

Memorial Wall

4. 5.6
40 feet. No anchors.
F.A. Unknown

5. Mossmouth 5.8 ★★
45 feet. Go up and to the right at the top. Would get 3 stars if not for the funky finish. This climb was bolted on lead, in the rain. 5 bolts plus anchors.
F.A. Nathan Smith, Greg Thompson. July 2002

6. Rain Maker 5.9 ★
40 feet. Hidden holds at the top. 5 bolts plus anchors.
F.A. Nathan Smith, Matt Sherry. July 2002

Ruth Lake

Nathan Smith on Skyler's Arete 5.11b, Ruth Lake

Matt Sherry on Mossmouth 5.8, Ruth Lake

IT IS POSSIBLE
Matt Fetcho, Omega Engineer
At Uinta Mountains, Utah
Omega Pacific
www.omegapac.com

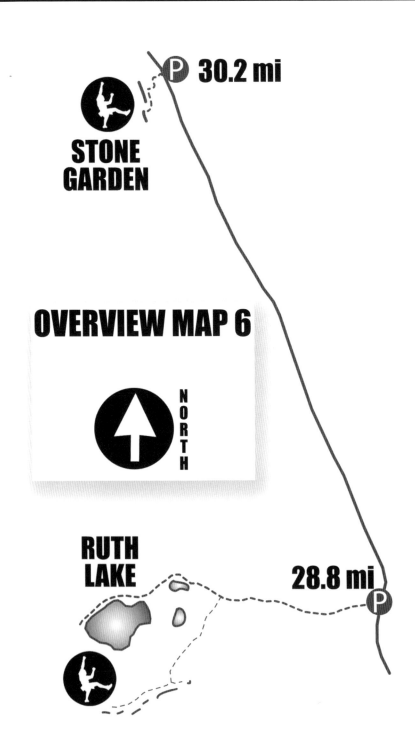

SULPHER CAMPGROUND

BOURBON PEAK

32.7 mi

30.8 mi

Stone Garden

Description: Offering a full range of climbing, the Stone Garden is home to the steepest routes on Uinta quartzite. The large roof is marked with beautiful black "tiger striped" black streaks and is in perpetual shade. The left side of the wall is in the sun until noon. Elevation: 10,000 ft.

Directions: About half a mile past mile marker 36 or 30.2 miles past the tollbooth, you will find a small pullout marked by a cairn on the east side of the road. There is a second pullout .1 miles further if the 1st pullout is full. The trail starts directly across from the parking area on the west side of the road. The hike will take 10 to 15 minutes. From Left to Right:
USGS Map: Hayden Peak and Mirror Lake

1. Here Today, Tomorrow & Next Week 5.10d ★★
40 feet. 5 bolts plus anchors.
F.A. Paul Moore, Shane Willet. Summer 1995

2. Laborious 5.11b ★
30 feet. A thin and bouldery start leads to easier climbing above. 5 bolts plus anchors.
F.A. Paul Moore, Shane Willet, Mark Nakada. Summer 1995

3. Fear of Gear 5.7 ★★
40 feet. A varying crack, this climb eats hexes and medium to large cams. Use smaller gear at the start. Bolted anchor.
F.A. Paul Moore. Summer 1995

4. F.Y.D. 5.10c ★
45 feet. A good slab that wanders right at the top. 6 bolts plus anchors.
F.A Mark Nakada, Shane Willet, Paul Moore. Summer 1995

5. Grief 5.8 ★
60 feet. 7 bolts plus anchors.
F.A. Shane Willet, Paul Moore. Summer 1995

6. Dilemma 5.10d
75 feet. Clip 2 bolts at the roof then all gear. A set of stoppers, gear to 1" and 24" runners will help you through.
F.A. Jonny Woodward. Summer 1995

7. Tortured Screams 5.10b ★★
75 feet. A fun roof leads to easier climbing above. 9 bolts plus anchors.
F.A. Shane Willet, Paul Moore, Mark Nakada. Summer 1995

Stone Garden

8. Tension and Stress 5.10c ★

75 feet. Similar to the others on the wall, a roof to easier climbing. 9 bolts plus anchors.

F.A. Shane Willet, Paul Moore, Mark Nakada. Summer 1995

9. Ceremonial Execution 5.10a ★

75 feet. Same start and finish as Tension and Stress, but go right at the shelf. 7 bolts plus anchors.

F.A. Shane Willet, Paul Moore, Mark Nakada. Summer 1995

10. Blah, Blah, Blah 5.10a

75 feet. Straight up the right-hand side of the wall. 6 bolts plus anchors.

F.A. Shane Willet, Paul Moore, Mark Nakada. Summer 1995

11. The Gentleman Who Fell 5.9

75 feet. The left-most route on the steep wall. 6 bolts plus anchors.

F.A. Shane Willet, Paul Moore, Mark Nakada. Summer 1995

12. Next Year 5.10d

75 feet. Gear to 1", bolted anchors.

F.A. Jonny Woodward. Summer 1995

13. Block Buster 5.11b ★★

75 feet. Gear to 1.5" interspersed with bolts.

F.A. Jonny Woodward. Summer 1995

14. Blood Sucker 5.12b

75 feet. Bolts and gear to 1.5". This line is hard to read.

F.A. Jonny Woodward. Summer 1995

15. Stink Bug 5.12d ★

50 feet. Gear to 1.5" Be prepared for a pump.

F.A. Jonny Woodward. Summer 1995

16. Large Chested Mutant 5.11d ★★

50 feet. Same start as Sessions then go left to Stink Bug's anchors. Gear to 1.5"

F.A. Martin Berzins, Jonny Woodward. Summer 1995

17. Sessions 5.12a ★★★★★
60 feet. The best route in the Uintas!!! Got endurance? 7 bolts plus anchors.
F.A. Fred Henion, Jonathan Knight, Shane Willet. Summer 1995

18. Hypoxia 5.12d ★
60 feet. Use a 2' draw on the bolt before you pull the roof. 6 bolts plus anchors.
F.A. Geoff Weigand. Summer 1997

19. Lost Souls 5.12b ★★
60 feet. This route would be 3-stars anywhere else, but is slightly diminished next to Sessions.
F.A. Fred Henion, bolted by Shane Willet, Paul Moore. Summer 1995

Stone Garden

Stone Garden

20. Married to the Obsessed 5.10d ★
45 feet. 9 bolts plus anchors.
F.A. Paul Moore, Shane Willet, Mark Nakada. Summer 1995

21. Charm (aka: Slappin' Em Down) 5.10d ★★
45 feet. Start at a small roof that looks harder than it is. 7 black painted bolts plus anchors.
F.A. Jeff Baldwin. Summer 2003

22. Cries of Impending Doom 5.11b ★★
45 feet. Continuous and pumpy all the way. 9 bolts plus anchors.
F.A. Shane Willet, Paul Moore, Mark Nakada. Summer 1995

23. Bloody Knuckles 5.7 ★
20 feet. You can place gear up to .75" for the start, then climb past 2 bolts to the anchors.
F.A. Shane Willet, Paul Moore. Summer 1995

24. The Birds From Hell 5.8 ★
20 feet. 3 bolts plus anchors.
F.A. Shane Willet, Paul Moore. Summer 1995

Stone Garden

Mushroom Wall

Directions: This small wall is to the left of the main wall, hidden in the trees. For climbs 6 - 10 follow the upper band of the cliff 200 yards left of Here Today, Tomorrow & Next Week. For Climbs 1 & 2, follow the lower cliff band to the boulderfield.

Description: This wall is short and bouldery with nice shady climbing all day long.

1. Use the Flat End 5.10c ★
20 feet. The left-bolted variation for the first "pitch" of Agrosbye or Water Club. 3 bolts plus anchors.
F.A. Dave Bollshweiler, Christien and Andy Knight.

2. Where's the Ladder ? 5.10b ★
20 feet. The easier right bolted variation for the first "pitch" of Agrosbye or Water Club. 3 bolts plus anchors.
F.A. Dave Bollshweiler, Christien and Andy Knight.

3. Water Club 5.10b ★
30 feet. Located on the far left of the upper tier. Climbs 1 and 2 can be used to access this pitch. 4 bolts plus anchors.
F.A. Lange Jeffries. Summer 1997

4. Agrosbye 5.11a ★★
30 feet. Climbs 1 and 2 can be used to access this pitch. 4 bolts plus anchors.
F.A. Dave Sanders Summer 1997

Uinta Rock

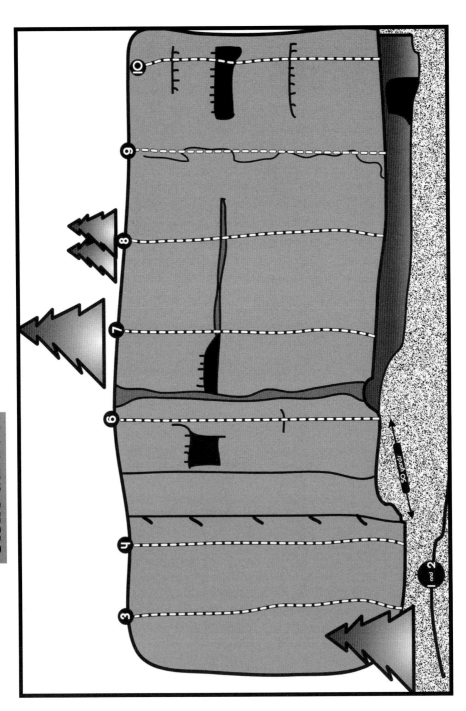

5. 5.9 TR
Toperope the dark corner.
F.A. Unknown

6. Clitocybe 5.11b ★
30 feet. A mixed route that uses .5 to 2 Camalots. 3 bolts. Walk off.
F.A. Lange Jeffries. Summer 1996

7. Orange Plasma 5.10c
30 feet. Clip the first bolt from the ground, and cruise past 4 more bolts to the tree anchor.
F.A. Lange Jeffries. Summer 1996

8. Lead Power 5.12b ★
25 feet. Short and bouldery with a hard start. 4 bolts plus anchors.
F.A. Lange Jeffries. Summer 1996

9. Caps 5.9 ★
25 feet. A varying crack. Bring a full-size range. Bolted anchors
F.A. Lange Jeffries. Summer 1997

10. Jack-O-Lantern 5.11a ★
25 feet. Good climbing with good rests. 4 bolts plus anchors
F.A. Lange Jeffries. Summer 1997

Stone Garden

Bourbon Peak

Bourbon Peak *(sidebar)*

Directions: You have 2 options for accessing these routes:
1. Park at the Bourbon Lake Trailhead. 32.7 miles from the toll-booth or just before mile marker 39. Hike the trail to the lake then to the routes on the cliffs above.
2. Using a 4WD road near mile marker 37 drive to a small parking lot. Hike a social trail to the lake then take the path of least resistance to the cliff.

Description: With routes 40 to 60 meters long and not a bolt in sight, this is an "adventure" crag. All routes use a standard rack and start on a large ledge system accessed by a pitch of 4th to easy 5th class climbing above a 30 to 40 degree slope. Dislodged rocks will roll all the way to the lake. Caution and a helmet are HIGHLY recommended as there is much loose rock. Walk off the wall to the climber's right.
Elevation: 10,200 ft.
USGS Map: Whitney Reservoir

1. Crotch Rocket 5.5 ★★
Inside Corner
F.A. James Taylor, Carl Begal, John Bolke. Summer 1993

2. The Angel's Third 5.9 R ★
Shallow inside corner. Very loose at the start. Be careful!
F.A. Brian Cabe, Dwight Curry. 8/9/03.

3. Knob Creek 5.7 ★
Inside corner.
F.A. Brian Cabe, Dwight Curry. 8/9/03.

4. Old Crow 5.7 ★
Face just right of #3.
F.A. Brian Cabe, Dwight Curry. 8/9/03.

5. On the Rocks 5.10 R/X
Climb the loose arete. Not recommended. VERY loose.
F.A. Brian Cabe, Dwight Curry. 8/9/03.

6. Maker's Mark 5.8 R/X
Climb the inside corner just below a loose block/column. Take care around the loose feature!
F.A. Brian Cabe, Dwight Curry. 8/9/03.

Bourbon Peak

Reference

Baldwin, Jeff: *A Rock Climbing Guide to the Uintas*, Self Published, Salt Lake City, UT. 2001. 52 pgs.

Boren, Kerry R, Boren, Lisa L: *The Gold of Carre – Shinob*, Bonneville Books, Springville, UT. 1998. 198 pgs.

Boren, Kerry R, Boren, Lisa L: *The Utah Gold Rush*, Council Press, Springville, UT. 2002. 246 pgs.

Davis, Mel, Veranth, John: *High Uinta Trails*, Wasatch Publishers, Salt Lake City, UT. 3rd Printing 1998. 160 pgs.

Hansen, Wallace R: *The Geologic Story of the Uinta Mountains*, US Geological Survey Bulletin 1291, 1975. 144 pgs.

Hensleigh, Christine: *The Mother Lode,* Salt Lake City Weekly, May 3, 2001.

Jones, Daniel J: *The Rocks and Scenery of Camp Steiner,* US Geological Survey Bulletin 51, 1955. 36 pgs.

Patterson, Scott: *Western Uinta Backcountry Guide*, Notch Mountain Publishing, Kearns UT. 103 pgs.

Probst, Jeffery, Probst, Brad: *High Uintas Backcountry – A Guide and Trip Planner*, Outland Publishing, Bountiful, UT. 1996. 293 pgs.

Shaw, Richard J: *Wildflowers of the Wasatch and Uinta Mountains*, Wheelwright Press, LTD., Salt Lake City, UT. 1976. 61 pgs.

Stokes, William L: *Geology of Utah*, Utah Museum of Natural History, University of Utah and Utah Geological and Mineral Survey, Department of Natural Resources, Salt Lake City, UT. Second Printing 1998. 280 pgs.

Index

Stone, Jim: *High Country Climbing, A Guide to Rock Climbing in the Uinta Mountains*. Self Published, Park City, UT.

Thompson, George A: *Faded Footprints – The Lost Rhoades Mines and Other Hidden Treasures of the Uintas*, Dream Garden Press, Salt Lake City, UT. Revised Edition 1996. 206 pgs.

Thompson, George A: *Lost Treasures on the Old Spanish Trail*, Western Epics, Salt Lake City, UT. 4th printing 1999. 122 pgs.

Compiled by: The Utah Society for Environmental Education: *A Guide to the Mirror Lake Scenic Byway.* 148 pgs.

Photo: Brian Cabe

Dwight Curry on The Angel's Third 5.9, Bourbon Peak

Index

Uinta Rock

5.4

5.5

5.6

5.7

5.8

Index

Index

Uinta Rock

5.10a

Index

Index

Uinto Rock

5.11b

- Block Buster 5.11b ★★ 175
- Cat Fud 5.11b ★★ 102
- Clitocybe 5.11b ★ 181
- Crash Test 5.11b R 30
- Cries of Impending Doom 5.11b ★★ 178
- Crumble Cake 5.11b ★★ 137
- Fehrris Buehler 5.11b ★★★ 89
- Got my Goat 5.11b ★★ 104
- Harmfull Variants 5.11b 97
- Laborious 5.11b ★ 172
- Mad Man of the Uintas 5.11b ★ 116
- Moon Stone 5.11b ★★ 154
- Realization 5.11b ★★ 97
- Skyler's Arete 5.11b ★ 166
- Spanish Love 5.11b 34
- The Shield 5.11b ★★★ 99
- The Sword 5.11b ★★ 99
- Tree Hugger 5.11b 51
- Vision Quest 5.11b 153
- Wall of Mirrors 5.11b 113

5.11b/c

- A Song and Dance 5.11b/c 56
- Shinangwav 5.11b/c ★★ 127

5.11c

- Alien's Face 5.11c ★★ 102
- All's Fehr 5.11c ★★ 89
- Brief Case 5.11c ★ 142
- Cry of the Warrior 5.11c R 162
- Dream Catcher 5.11c ★★ 153
- Fehr Thee Well 5.11c ★★ 89
- Fist Full of Scalps 5.11c ★★ 161
- Forgotten Warrior 5.11c ★ 156
- Gary's Cows 5.11c ★★ 102
- Ray of Light 5.11c ★ 115
- Stay Free 5.11c R ★★ 97
- Utahpia 5.11c ★ 97
- Utahpia Variation 5.11c 97

- Wind Walker 5.11c ★★ 153

5.11d

- Corporate Hippy 5.11d ★★ 131
- Dog Man 5.11d ★★★ 163
- Fehra Fawcet 5.11d ★★ 89
- Large Chested Mutant 5.11d ★★ 175
- Lost Wages 5.11d ★★ 105
- Mid Day Lighting Direct 5.11d 63
- Modest Yuppie 5.11d ★★ 132
- Pro Coffee Yes 5.11d ★★ 56
- Tipping the Vessel of Knowledge 5.11d ★★★ 83
- Vinegar of Hostility 5.11d ★★ 83

5.12

- Corporate Soldier 5.12 ★★ 132
- Modest Soldier 5.12 ★★ 132
- Pink Hippy 5.12 ★★ 131
- Test of Time 5.12 100

5.12a

- .38 Special 5.12a ★ 140
- Good Medicine 5.12a ★★ 153
- Harsh Reality 5.12a ★ 125
- Orange Crush 5.12a ★★★ 101
- Pink Soldier 5.12a ★★ 131
- Sessions 5.12a ★★★★★ 176
- Spirit Guide 5.12a 153
- The Death of Democracy 5.12a R ★ 140

5.12b

- Blood Sucker 5.12b 175
- Ghost Dance 5.12b ★★★ 154
- Grit 5.12b X 113
- Lead Power 5.12b ★ 181
- Lost Souls 5.12b ★★ 176
- Tequilla 5.12b ★★ 116
- Warrior Without a Cause 5.12b ★★ 163

5.12b/c

5.12c/d

5.12d

5.12+

Index

About the Authors

Nathan Smith

Nathan is a local climber/photographer whose work has been published in Climbing, Rock & Ice, She Sends and the Utah Sportsguide as well as used by many outdoor companies for advertising and catalog usage. He has been climbing for 12 years and has over 50 sport, trad, ice and mixed first ascents in Utah. Nathan is also the co author/publisher of Wasatch Mixed, a mixed rock/ice climbing guide to the Wasatch Mountains, written with Doug Heinrich.

Paul Tusting

Paul grew up climbing in New England, but has lived in Utah since 1999. Since moving to Salt Lake City, he has worked full time in the outdoor industry, engineering, testing, and designing new equipment. His technical writing has been published in several climbing catalogs, magazines, and presented in a technical rescue symposium. Over the last four years he has become enthralled with developing new climbing areas and has been involved in well over one hundred first ascents in the Intermountain West.

Index